Everyday Letters *for* Busy People

REVISED EDITION

Hundreds of Samples You Can Adapt at a Moment's Notice:

- *Invitations and Resignations*
- *Complaints and Condolences*
- *E-mail and Snail Mail*
- *and more*

Debra Hart May
and
Regina McAloney

CAREER
PRESS

EVERYDAY LETTERS FOR BUSY PEOPLE, REVISED EDITION
EDITED BY CLAYTON W. LEADBETTER
TYPESET BY EILEEN DOW MUNSON
Cover design by Foster & Foster, Inc.
Printed in the U.S.A. by Book-mart Press

To order this title, please call toll-free 1-800-CAREER-1 (NJ and Canada: 201-848-0310) to order using VISA or MasterCard, or for further information on books from Career Press.

The Career Press, Inc., 3 Tice Road, PO Box 687,
Franklin Lakes, NJ 07417
www.careerpress.com

Library of Congress Cataloging-in-Publication Data

May, Debra Hart, 1961-
   Everyday letters for busy people : hundreds of samples you can adapt at a moment's notice : invitations and resignations, complaints and condolences, e-mail and snail mail, and more / by Debra Hart May & Regina McAloney.— Rev. ed.
     p. cm.
   Includes index.
   ISBN 1-56414-712-6 (pbk.)
   1. English language—Rhetoric—Handbooks, manuals, etc. 2. Letter writing—Handbooks, manuals, etc. 3. Form letters—Handbooks, manuals, etc. I. McAloney, Regina. II. Title.

PE1483.M32 2004
808.6—dc22

2003061324

To Debra's husband,
Mark,
and to Regina's grandmother,
Josephine,
a devoted letter writer.

Contents

Sample Letters and E-mail Messages

Why Read This Book?

Many books give you advice about how to write a good letter. A lot of books even offer sample letters from which you can borrow lines or use in their entirety. This book, however, not only offers advice and lots of sample letters, it gives you tips and samples that fit realistic, familiar occasions for writing a letter—from personal business (such as expressing a complaint, writing to the editor of a publication, or inquiring about insurance) to social concerns (such as making an announcement, expressing regret, or extending an invitation).

This book also helps you answer one of the most pressing questions in this age of electronic communication: When is it appropriate, or perhaps more worthwhile, to send electronic mail instead of a letter? We not only answer this question but supply you with sample e-mail messages designed to engage their recipients and get results. In fact, all of the samples in this book were crafted not to be flowery or clever, but to help you accomplish your purpose for writing in the first place. We figure that if you're taking the time to pull a letter together (or just to find the right ready-made letter), you want it to be effective.

Beyond that, if writing is a task you find challenging or don't enjoy, you've picked the right book. This book offers much more than samples, which, let's face it, may not always work for you; it provides suggestions that can help you fly solo. When you need to write all or just a part of a letter or e-mail message on your own, this book can help in four ways:

1. It provides templates, or step-by-step guidelines, for composing different types of letters or e-mails. Whatever your situation, the corresponding template can help you decide how to begin, develop, and end a truly effective message.

2. Marginal notes next to each sample letter or e-mail help you see how the sample conforms to a particular template.

3. Checklists help you make sure you've covered aspects critical to succeeding with each type of letter or e-mail.

4. A simple five-step formula helps you quickly decide—before you be-
    gin writing—what you want your letter or e-mail to accomplish and
    what the recipient will most want to read.

Please note that all of the names, addresses, zip codes, phone numbers, and
scenarios used in the samples in this book are fictitious. Only the addresses of U.S.
government agencies are real. (Names of government officials, however, are not.)
Also note that the sample letters appear in the format appropriate for stationery
without letterhead. When you use letterhead, omit your name and address if the
sample directs you to include them.

Whether you decide to use parts of the samples that this book provides or
start from scratch, the advice that follows can help you get the most out of the
time you spend writing a letter or typing an e-mail.

CHAPTER 1

When Is a Letter the Best Way to Communicate?

Hardly anyone writes letters anymore. Most of us, when we need to voice a complaint, express appreciation, or handle almost any personal business matter, either pick up the phone or log into our e-mail account. Typically, placing a call takes less time and effort than sitting down to compose a letter. What's more, e-mail has all but replaced letter-writing, and even phone calls, as the standard way to communicate quickly with customer service departments, product manufacturers, government entities, and organizations of all sorts. In fact, to instantly post what we need to say, we can usually just click a "Contact us" button on these organizations' Websites.

Social situations, too, seem to simply require a telephone call or a text message. And what about sending an e-card, an e-invitation, or a social announcement by e-mail? At the most, a regular greeting card is enough, isn't it? After all, hardly a social situation exists for which we can't find a card these days. But before you click on that "Send" button or visit the local card shop, here are a few things to consider.

The changing status of letters

The swiftness and ease of e-mails and phone calls, not to mention the fact that they don't require postage, seem to have diminished the role of letter-writing in modern life. Job seekers now transmit resumes and thank-you notes via the Internet; family members send one another e-greetings for holidays, special occasions, or just to say "Hi"; brides and grooms broadcast rehearsal night details with the help of mass e-mails. Indeed, e-mail, pagers, text messaging, faxes, and phones have taken the hassle and cost out of many a task.

On the other hand, the popularity of electronic communication has also given letter-writing a newfound privileged status. In some situations, no electronic message says "business" the way a signed, carefully crafted memo on official letterhead can. Nor does e-mail express emotion and personality the way our penmanship and personal stationery can. What we gain in formality and artistry, we sometimes lose in convenience.

Here are some pointers to help you determine when a letter or e-mail is better than a phone call—and when that "old-fashioned" letter may be the best thing of all!

The advantages of putting your message in writing

For starters, handling personal business by phone doesn't always work. In some situations, letters or e-mails are more practical.

- One phone call often becomes several, as you're passed from one person (or worse, voice-mail message) to the next, stating your need or complaint multiple times. Then you wait for a return call from that one person, who is the only one allowed to help you (and she's out of the office...).

- In some situations, and with some organizations regardless of the situation, no number of phone calls will result in the action you need. Government entities, for instance, often require a form or letter to document the issue at hand prior to their taking any action.

- If you're in *any* situation that requires documenting what you've said and the responses you've received, it's handy to have hard copies or electronic files on your side. For instance, you may need to track what a company promised about an order that was shipped too late.

- A call can be impractical and inconvenient when the business at hand is important but not urgent. For example, you might just want to tell a political candidate about your views on an environmental issue.

- A call can be troublesome when the information is complicated and likely to be misunderstood, lost, or miscommunicated. When a complicated situation fails to be resolved with a first or second phone call, you're typically better off putting pen to paper or typing away on your keyboard.

- Past experience with an organization may tell you that only a formal letter, less easily ignored than a phone call, will result in action. And a letter is typically the only way to make your appeal to anyone even close to the CEO.

- Many employers prefer receiving communications with job candidates via the post office or electronic mail. They'd rather be free of the nuisance of phone inquiries by persistent job seekers, or of voice mailboxes filled to maximum capacity.

- A call can be intrusive for a stressed recipient—for instance, someone struggling with a business deadline.

- A call can be awkward or inappropriate when someone is grieving the loss of a loved one, dealing with personal tragedy, or involved in some other private matter about which you may not be aware.

- A call may not be best when you are angry or suspect a recipient might respond with defensiveness (as with a complaint) or embarrassment (as with a compliment or congratulations).

The advantages of putting your message in a *letter*

In some cases, neither a phone call, an e-mail message, or even a card is formal or lasting enough, whether for business or social purposes.

- A call or e-mail message expresses too casual a message when your purpose is formal or your intent deeply heartfelt. Only a letter or note may really work for an invitation to a charity event you wish to promote, a thank-you for an overnight stay, or an expression of sympathy when someone has died. A card can sometimes express the sentiment you're looking for, but often only something more elaborate—a letter—will do.

- Because e-mail *is* so quick and convenient, it sometimes leaves the impression—particularly during a job search and in delicate social circumstances—that not much thought or effort was involved on your part. The care you spend in selecting the right stationery and typeface for your cover letter or creatively decorating your letter to a dear friend will not go unnoticed.

- Calls and electronic messages cannot always provide the kind of formal documentation you or your reader may want for future reference. Examples include: documentation of details that require privacy, such as identification numbers, medical claim data, or account information; receipts for service and copies of legal documents; a reference or formal introduction to a colleague; a job acceptance, rejection, or resignation; and information on successive attempts to collect money or obtain compensation.

- Add to all of this the fact that e-mail has gained a reputation for being a forum for poor English, cryptic abbreviations, "emoticons," annoying chain letters, trifling or offensive jokes and attachments, unsolicited marketing messages ("spam"), and computer viruses. It's clear that your formal, sealed letter will be more often appreciated than not!

Of course, e-mail has its advantages, too...

- Most employers are looking for job candidates who aren't intimidated by e-mail or posting their resumes online. Many employers even request that you send your cover letter and resume *only* to their e-mail address. Not only does doing this demonstrate how technology-savvy you are, but it allows employers quick access to your information and the ability to log any of your communications and attachments into their computer filing system. (See Chapter 2, however, for precautions on career-related e-mailing.)

- Many companies and organizations, especially those with a strong online ordering or customer-service component, operate almost completely in the world of cyberspace. They expect you to contact them by e-mail, and they *will* respond to you promptly. Why draft a letter to that online merchant when you can send your question with the click of a mouse?

☞ When something unexpected occurs at the last minute (for example, a change in the venue or time of a get-together, or the need to clarify some driving directions that you sent with an invitation), the time constraints involved almost *demand* that you send a group e-mail if you happen to have all the necessary e-mail addresses on hand.

☞ And, of course, when you're completing a project or a report on a deadline, the post office cannot surpass the time-saving ability of e-mail.

If we've just reinforced what you've always valued about e-mail, we want to stress that there are definite guidelines for crafting elegant and effective e-mail messages. There are also situations in which you might want to opt for a message that's signed, sealed, and delivered rather than propelled into the wonderful world of wireless, and you need to know how to figure out when that's the case. Be sure to read Chapter 2, "Advice and Etiquette for E-mail Enthusiasts."

The benefits of a well-written letter

Sometimes composing a good letter is both the most effective and the most expedient way to express a message or get something done. What's more, a well-crafted letter can allow you to express yourself more carefully and clearly than you're probably able to on the fly (whether on the phone, in a card, or by e-mail). And letters, without equal, make a strong impression: Your words, when put in letter form, carry more weight than those conveyed either by phone, card, or computer. So once you've decided to write a letter, **take the time to write it well**. Poorly written letters are often guilty of putting off their readers.

☞ Letters of complaint tend to ramble through a long chronology of events and often bury or fail to even express the writer's point: the action wanted of the reader!

☞ Letters on emotionally-charged topics often wallow in emotion and fail to clearly express their point.

☞ Letters written with the slightest hint of anger or sarcasm—even when the writers feel fully justified in their positions—divert attention from the real issue, confuse the facts of a situation with feelings and personal attacks, make cooperation less likely, and can jeopardize long-standing relationships.

☞ Letters saying no often offend readers by containing one-sided, excuse-ridden, or politely elusive explanations.

Well-written letters, on the other hand, can go a long way to build relationships, assist others in solving problems, ease tense situations, clarify or verify important information, and motivate others to act!

CHAPTER 2

Advice and Etiquette for E-mail Enthusiasts

Yes, e-mail is fast. And yes, it allows you to send the same message to many people at once. And, of course, you can send an e-mail at any time of the day or night and know it will reach its intended recipient in a matter of minutes (that is, as long as you've typed the correct e-mail address and all hardware is functioning properly). Additionally, you can be more conversational in e-mail than you might be in a formal letter.

But with all this convenience and ease, we tend to forget that composing a good e-mail requires thought and attention, just as writing a good letter does—especially when we have something important to say. We may also forget that e-mail may not be appropriate for some situations at all.

Writing a good e-mail doesn't have to be difficult, though. Neither does figuring out when to send a letter instead of an e-mail. That's why this chapter gives you simple tools for deciding when to use e-mail, as well as for crafting polite and effective e-mails with ease. Because good e-mail–writing involves many of the same principles that apply to good letter-writing, we also recommend that you read the chapters we've devoted to letter-writing—they discuss e-mail, as well.

Tips for deciding when to use e-mail

In the introduction and the previous chapter, we gave you a basic overview of the different perceptions people might have when you send an e-mail message instead of a letter. While there is no established "right" way to determine when a letter is more appropriate than e-mail, or vice versa, you may find the following formula helpful. It's called the "SNAIL" formula, inspired by the term "snail mail"—a popular name for traditional paper mail that has arisen because traditional mail takes longer than e-mail.

Using the SNAIL formula
to choose between e-mail and "snail mail"

If any of the following SNAIL characteristics describe (or *ought to* describe) the kind of message you're sending, you should probably put your message in a letter instead of an e-mail. A brief explanation of each characteristic follows this list.

Secure

Noted

Affective (not the same as *effective*)

Impressive

Legal

Secure

There is no such thing as private e-mail. We repeat: There is no such thing as private e-mail. No matter what fancy encryption options your e-mail system features, do not send anyone confidential details and issues via e-mail—especially if you're at work, referring to a monetary account, or noting any kind of personal identification number. In some e-mail systems, an administrator has the ability to read every e-mail that passes through. Employers, in particular, monitor their e-mail systems to be sure that employees are spending their time on company matters and keeping proprietary information confidential.

Aside from all this, a computer glitch (or a user error) may cause your "private" message to be sent to the wrong person. Also, although it's nice to think the best of everyone, don't assume your recipient won't *forward* your message to the wrong person, even if you've instructed him or her not to. Remember, the ease and speed of e-mail, as well as the likelihood of an immediate response, increase the possibility that your message—intentionally or not—may end up in the hands of an unintended recipient. And then, there are always hackers, who can, in theory, break into any e-mail account.

So, when it comes to sending e-mail—whether you're sending it from home, work, or the local library—don't send anything that you wouldn't want posted outside of City Hall, uploaded to a Website, or displayed on the company bulletin board. This means that messages requiring you to list secure account information (such as credit card numbers or PIN codes) or to release sensitive personal details (such as how many times you've visited the psychiatrist) are better off arriving at their destination in a stamped, sealed envelope.

Noted

By "noted" we mean "documented." While e-mail can be a written record of facts, dates, times, and events, its disadvantage is that it's electronic. Transmissions of data that require documentation can be lost because of software or hardware error. E-mail users can even change, falsify, or manipulate data in an existing e-mail by simply typing over the original text. Of course, you can always print your own hard copy of your message, but that doesn't mean the recipient of your e-mail will print or even save what you've sent.

When your message needs to alert someone to an update in important information, make a formal announcement of a life-changing event, or be accompanied by attachments, such as notarized or signed certificates, you will need to send a letter so that all parties involved have hard copies of authentic records to file away. For example, you wouldn't want to announce a change in an employee's job category or salary, register a new married name with the Social Security Administration, claim your deceased spouse's pension benefits, send important receipts, submit an invoice for payment, or extend an offer of employment through e-mail. Also, even though you can always scan records or certificates and attach the electronic file to an e-mail, most organizations and individuals will request the "genuine article."

Affective

Affective is another word for "emotional" or "sensitive." When it's really important that your recipient sense a certain kind of emotion behind your words, such as sympathy or gratitude, a letter or a handwritten note is often the best way to go. There are a few reasons for this.

In e-mail, as in letters, you can't use facial expressions, gestures, or vocal inflections to show your feelings as you would in a face-to-face conversation. Even phone calls can convey more emotion. In e-mail, however, people do convey emotions by using *emoticons*, which are symbols created using the keyboard characters. For example, to express happiness, one would type a colon, a dash, and a close parenthesis mark, which results in the symbol of a smiley face—like so :-). However, even emoticons that symbolize "serious" feelings can leave the impression that you're being irreverent or cutesy, which is a bad thing if you're writing about a sensitive topic, such as the death of someone close to you.

Another difference between e-mail and letters is that what you see when composing a message may not be the same as what your reader sees. The software and hardware you use may not be the same as those of your correspondent, so any formatting and special visual enhancements you've added to convey a feeling or sentiment may be lost or distorted in transmission.

In addition, you can type something that would sound perfectly harmless in conversation but could be interpreted as sarcastic or accusatory in an e-mail. Your recipient may not be able to tell if you're sincere, serious, or kidding without the context that nice stationery or friendly handwriting can establish. And if you tend to express your emotions in writing by using exclamation points, capitalization, or other punctuation, your e-mail will give the impression that you're shouting, or even crazy!

Further, because e-mail can be so easily transmitted to unintended recipients, it isn't the right place to express certain emotions, such as anger or resentment.

Impressive

To state the obvious, when something is *impressive*, it makes an impression. If you seek to make a distinct impression with your message, a letter is the best medium. This is because our culture is heavily influenced by symbols. The elegant textured paper of a formal wedding invitation gives an impression of ceremony. A sheet of formal company letterhead gives an impression of respect and officiousness.

So, for example, if you want your resume and cover letter to stand out, send them on quality-stock paper via snail mail, as long as your prospective employer hasn't requested otherwise. By the same token, if you want to tell your Aunt Susan that her presence at your barbecue meant the world to you, a handwritten letter on attractive stationery will command her appreciation more than *yet one more e-mail* she has to open.

Legal

Perhaps it goes without saying that issues pertaining to contracts, legal obligations, and other legal matters, such as a notice to evict or a request for leniency, should be signed, dated, and submitted by mail. For very important letters, keep in mind that "read receipts" are not just the domain of e-mail; getting a confirmation that your letter has been received is possible with "snail mail," too, for a nominal fee.

One final note: If you've applied the SNAIL formula and still aren't sure whether you should send an e-mail or a letter, by all means, send a letter, especially if you have any hesitation at all about transmitting your message via the information superhighway.

E-mail do's and don'ts

So, you've ruled out snail mail and you're about to log into your e-mail account. Before you start typing, remember these pointers, which will help you compose a message that will invite your reader's respect and response:

1. **Don't type in all caps**. As previously mentioned, this is perceived as shouting.

2. **Don't write a novel.** A university study recently showed that people are perceived as *more* intelligent when their writing is simple and to the point. Multisyllabic words, descriptive clauses, and long paragraphs, instead of proclaiming your genius, apparently turn off your reader. Never write more than what would amount to one typewritten page, and limit your line length to 65–70 characters across. (You may need to adjust your e-mail program's setting for wrapping lines.) E-mail that requires endless scrolling to read will eventually lose its recipient's attention, especially if he or she has logged on via an expensive dial-up connection.

3. **Do carefully consider what you write or attach.** Your e-mail is a permanent record that can be easily forwarded to others.

4. **Do begin your e-mails with a salutation.** Don't launch right into your complaint, issue, or whatever it may be without demonstrating courtesy by formally addressing your reader. If your recipient is familiar to you, such as a close friend or friendly acquaintance, a "Hi, Rick" or "Dear Emilia" is fine. In e-mails of a nonsocial nature, you should begin your e-mail with the same kind of headers and addresses that you would normally include if you were sending the same message by regular mail (see Chapters 5 and 6, "The Parts of a Letter" and "Forms of Address"). This rule, of course, applies when your recipient is not a familiar coworker whose headers would be the same as yours. (See "Precautions on career-related e-mail" on page 19.)

5. **Don't attach large files or files created on uncommon software** without getting permission from your recipient first.

6. **Do type the** http:// **prefix before any Website address** you include in your message. This will enable most e-mail users to link to the Web address directly from the e-mail message.

7. **Don't send unsolicited advertisements and promotions.** This is called "spam," and most people block it and/or report it to their e-mail administrator. Spam will do nothing to enhance the reputation of your business.

8. **Do make your reply, or any of your comments, clear and easy to find** in the body of your message. When you open an e-mail to reply to it or to forward it, some e-mail programs automatically set your cursor at the end of any original messages. It is annoying for readers to have to scroll down through blocks of text to find your message (that is, if they can even recognize that you have written something). So be sure to move your cursor to the start of your message before you reply. Also, don't include an entire original message if you're responding to only a couple of its points. Briefly reference the items stated in the original text. And if you're answering questions, don't bury your responses within the text of the original message. Number your responses to correspond to the questions, or briefly refer to each question.

9. **Don't use the jargon and acronyms** that have become part of text messaging and e-mail lingo unless your e-mail is very casual and you know for certain your recipient uses the same lingo. The time you try to save time by typing *BTW* instead of *By the way* or *B/C* for *because* may result in greater time spent by your reader trying to figure out what you mean. And don't use this lingo *at all* in messages of a nonsocial nature.

10. **Do ask permission before forwarding a message**, unless you have been told that the message was meant to be shared.

11. **Do proofread your e-mail before you send it.** In fact, read it twice. E-mail may be considered an informal way to communicate, but that doesn't mean it should

be ridden with typos and grammatical errors that will confound recipients and make you look bad. Make sure your spelling is correct; take special care to spell recipients' names correctly. Don't rely too heavily on your spell-checker, though, because it won't hesitate to turn unfamiliar personal names into proper nouns such as *Ethiopia* and *January*.

12. **Do include your "signature" in business or noncasual e-mails.** Like a signature on paper, a signature in e-mail can appear at the end of your message. But unlike a signature on paper, a signature in the world of e-mail is really a form of letterhead. It typically displays your name, title, address, and other contact information. To automatically append a signature to the end of your outgoing messages, you will need to access the "signature" feature in your e-mail program and type in the information you'd like to display. Limit your signature to five lines, or you'll end up with too much information for your reader that just makes you look like you think you're very important. Signatures can be an invaluable tool in the workforce, because they usually include the phone number(s) at which you can be reached.

13. **Don't overdo it with formatting, designs, and clip art.** As mentioned previously, what you see on screen may not be the same thing your reader sees, so you could be just wasting your time.

14. **Don't compose e-mail messages in hypertext markup language (HTML).** Composing an HTML message means your e-mail will be delivered to most people with an attachment that is an exact duplicate of your original message but contains colors and formatting meant to be viewed with an Internet browser, such as Internet Explorer or Netscape Navigator. Make sure your e-mail program is set to send "simple" or "text-only" messages instead of "HTML." Look under the "tools," "options," or "preferences" menu in your e-mail program to make this adjustment.

15. **Don't send chain letters**—by e-mail or by snail mail. No one likes to be told that he or she will have 10 years of bad luck if the "Teddy Bear Prayer" is not forwarded to 12 friends.

16. **Don't overpunctuate.** Refrain from using ellipses (three periods in a row), too many exclamation points, or several question marks in a row. Ellipses are meant to signify an omission in a direct quotation—not trailing thoughts. Exclamation points are meant for *occasional* emphasis. Otherwise, they make an e-mail look as if a very "Type-A" person has written it. Several question marks in a row look like a demand for an answer.

17. **Do make consumer complaint or inquiry e-mails concise and complete.** Provide the information in your message that the organization requests. Check the company's Website FAQ (Frequently Asked Questions) section to find out what details you need to give. Be sure to follow the advice in this book for making complaint letters brief and effective. (See the section "Consumer Letters and E-mails" on page 134.)

18. Do refrain from sending the same thank-you or friendly e-mail to a horde of friends at once. Unless you're planning an informal get-together with friends who you know check their e-mail every day, you're better off calling, sending a note, or at least sending each person an individual e-mail. Some people are put off by mass e-mails because they are often used to forward trite jokes and stories and because they seem *too easy* to send. Your thank-you will look like a task you just needed to get out of the way. Mass e-mails lack the personal touch that a letter, or at least a card, can provide.

As a general rule, when it comes to writing e-mail, let "less is more" be your guiding principle.

Precautions on career-related e-mail

We've explained the ins and outs of writing e-mail in general. Rules of etiquette become a little more complex in the workplace, where, most of the time, anything you do or say can, and probably will, be held against your job performance record. It is still important to write your business memos and reports well, whether you put them in e-mail or on paper. Job seekers, too, need to take special care in drafting their correspondence to prospective employers via e-mail. Here are some tips:

Before sending a resume, confirm that your prospective employer has the right software to open the kind of files that you're sending.

Always type your recipient's e-mail address into the "To" field *last*. This should be the very last step before you send your message. You should complete your e-mail, proofread it carefully, and only then fill in the "To" field, when you're absolutely ready to hit "Send." This will help you avoid sending a message that is missing an attachment or an important paragraph, filled with errors, or addressed to the wrong person.

When composing a cover letter by e-mail, include the proper salutation, headers, and addresses. (See Chapter 5, "The Parts of a Letter" and Chapter 6, "Forms of Address," as well as the section "Job and Career Letters and E-mails" on page 95.) Also, be sure to include your contact information in the body of your message, whether in your e-mail signature or in a closing statement.

Always double-check files after attaching them to your message. Open them up after attaching them. Check whether you've attached the correct version of your file, or even the right file at all—whether this is a resume or another work-related file.

Know the company's e-mail policy. Most organizations that use e-mail have a written statement of rules regarding the proper use of company e-mail. If the company does not have such a statement, refer to any statements the organization may have regarding the proper use of its resources and communications systems, and use your best judgment.

Treat an e-mail as though it were a printed memo. An e-mail can be as legally binding as a paper document. Especially if your e-mail correspondence is with a person outside of your organization, do not send anything by e-mail that you would not send as a memo or a letter.

Be careful if your e-mail deals with sensitive or proprietary company information. When you correspond with someone outside of the organization, you represent the organization—not just yourself. The organization may be held responsible for the statements in your e-mail. Some statements should never be transmitted by e-mail, either internally or externally. Always check with someone knowledgeable in your organization before sending an e-mail that addresses sensitive information.

Make sure there is nothing in your e-mail that can come back to haunt you. Do not include or refer to workplace rumors, gossip, or other issues not directly related to business. Before sending an e-mail, ask yourself whether you'd be in any kind of trouble if the whole organization read what you wrote.

Be careful about sending jokes or using humor. If your reader is offended by the content of your e-mail or its attachment, you could be accused of workplace harassment. Aside from that, your e-mail could be forwarded to someone inside or outside the organization with whom you would rather not share it. This can be embarrassing and damaging to your reputation. Also, always remember that employers routinely archive e-mail and monitor their e-mail systems.

Avoid sending personal e-mail using your workplace e-mail account. Most organizations include rules on sending personal e-mail within their company e-mail policy.

Above all, use common sense when you're sending e-mail at work. As electronic mail continually evolves, new pitfalls and risks present themselves in the workplace. It is better to be cautious.

In conclusion, e-mail is a valuable tool in the workplace and life in general. Although it's electronic, e-mail is a form of print communication, just as a letter is. So you need your e-mail to demonstrate that, in writing it, you've considered that there is going to be someone reading and responding to it. Therefore, you need to communicate clearly, cleanly, and with courtesy. The remaining chapters of this book will help guide you through this process and make your writing a success!

Tips for Drafting a Letter Quickly

Writing a good letter or e-mail takes thought. But it needn't be difficult or take a lot of time. Whether you decide to use pieces of the sample letters or e-mails we've provided in this book or to start your letter from scratch, you'll want to start the letter in a way to increase your likelihood of success.

British political scientist Graham Wallas (1858–1932) once said, "How do I know what I think until I see what I say?" Through writing about a subject, we become clear about what we think about that subject.

So before you draft the first word of your letter or e-mail—or begin to identify a suitable sample—start by doing some advanced thinking on paper or your computer.

If you don't, the sample letter or e-mail you choose as the model for your letter may miss the mark. Also, if you're drafting from scratch, your draft will probably be more difficult to write and, chances are, it will drag your reader through your thought process until your point, or purpose for writing in the first place, evolves on paper or on screen. And there's no surer way to make someone crazy—or at least impatient with what you have to say.

Think about the last piece of junk mail or e-mail that you actually read that took forever to get to the point. If you did choose to continue reading (perhaps you had nothing better to do at the moment), did you feel your time was being respected? Were you motivated to cooperate or buy the product? Or did you feel impatient, frustrated, even insulted?

Say you're thinking of writing a complaint letter or e-mail. Your first impulse may be to start it by spinning out your sad story, event by event. But what's your real goal here? If you're like most people, you want the wrong made right. Perhaps you even want an apology. That's where your letter should start—asking for what you want. After all, this is what you most need to communicate (this is typically the point behind this type of letter), and this is what the reader of your letter first wants to know! Think about it: If you were in his or her place, would you really want to blindly start reading a chronological listing of sad events? You'd want to first know why this person was writing to you. Then, perhaps, you'd be ready for the details.

To summarize: Both you and the recipient of your letter or e-mail need to get the letter's point, its bottom-line message, up front. And you can get to your point quickly in a letter only after you've thought through what your point is!

Getting started—especially if you don't like to write!

The following guidelines will help you begin to develop your e-mail or letter. Please note that e-mail writing is not appropriate for every type of writing situation described in this chapter or throughout this book. (Refer to Chapters 1 and 2 for details.) Because e-mail may not be suitable in all cases, we will be referring primarily to letters and letter-writing in the discussions of various writing situations that follow. But you can—and should—apply *any* of our advice to writing an e-mail, as long as you have determined, hopefully using the SNAIL method in Chapter 2, that e-mail is the right medium for your message.

That said, before you begin writing *any* kind of message, doing some advanced thinking on paper or on-screen brainstorming can help make the writing go more easily and quickly, even if you don't like to write!

Some people have no difficulty throwing together a basic letter, especially when the objective is straightforward, noncontroversial, and easy to get on paper or type up quickly. You want to return a defective product, get information about a charity you're interested in, or document stop payment on a bank check. These letters take little time or effort for many people who draft them quickly using an easy, free-flowing process.

But other kinds of letters are tougher to write. Maybe you need to write a complaint about receiving poor service from a favorite store, disappoint a good friend by declining an offer, or resign your position at work. These letters are harder to write and take more thought to write well. Many people struggle with these types of letters.

And some people find the process of writing a letter, any letter, nothing short of painful. If you ever find writing difficult, unpleasant, or just too time-consuming, consider for a moment *how you're approaching it.*

How are you going to write a letter? Is your approach to simply start with the first line, first word, and struggle along until it's done, in basically one draft? Are you thinking you want that draft to be as close to finished as possible so rewriting won't take up even more time and energy? Many people spend entirely too much time struggling to write a perfect first draft (an impossible task). Writing a solid, well-thought-out letter—especially when the subject's a tough one—involves several advanced-thinking steps, none of which should take much time.

Or maybe your approach is to scan a book like this for the perfect sample after which to model your letter. Certainly using a sample may save you some writing time—if you pick the best sample. But, again, do some advanced thinking first. You'll be clearer about where you want the letter to go, and you'll pick the best-suited model.

Your goal here is to change *the way you begin to write* to save yourself time *and* produce better letters. One trick is to spend more time doing this advanced thinking and less time—yes, less time—drafting.

Believe it or not, taking these advanced-thinking steps before you draft or look for a sample helps most people pull the actual letter together more quickly and easily.

A better writing process

So how do you go about this advanced thinking? The process we use involves five steps. Think in terms of CABGO.

Clarify your purpose.

Analyze your audience.

Brainstorm your ideas on the subject.

Group like ideas.

Order your groups of ideas.

Even if you plan to use a sample letter or e-mail in this book as your guide, use these steps to help you more quickly customize the sample you choose to best suit your needs. Both the samples and the letter templates will be most useful to you after you've done this thinking.

By the way, with even the toughest letter, this process should take you no more than 10 or 15 minutes.

Clarify your purpose

Many people start writing before they're really clear about what they're trying to accomplish. Then, almost invariably, they end up expressing the point of the letter toward its end—after it has already tried the reader's patience.

Upon first reading a letter, especially a long one, most readers typically think:

"Okay, what is this, and why should I read it?"

"Convince me this is important—I'm busy."

"This looks lengthy. How does it concern me?"

"Well, I don't have time now. What's it about—bottom line?"

As much as you'd like your readers to hang on to your every word, research shows that most people scan for only what's relevant *to them*.

So getting focused up front is critical. Before you write your first word of a rough draft, write a purpose statement. This statement, which will probably be different in your draft, should be a sentence or two that clearly and concisely states what you want to accomplish by writing this letter. A well-focused purpose statement very often describes not only *the point of the communication*, but also *the action you want the reader to take*.

23

Here's a worksheet you may want to use to help you clarify your thinking:

Purpose worksheet

The purpose of this letter is to:

_____

_____
(State purpose for writing)

so that _____
(Intended reader[s])

will _____

_____
(State action reader[s] should take)

Examples:

> *The purpose of this letter is to voice my complaints about problems I've had using this new software so that the manufacturer will either address these problems or refund my purchase price.*

> *The purpose of this letter is to introduce new meeting procedures so that civic committee members will come to the next meeting prepared to get things done more efficiently.*

Coming up with a concise purpose statement isn't always easy. If it doesn't come right away, we use a trick called "free-writing."

Free-writing: Thinking through to your point

Free-writing involves taking a blank sheet of paper or opening up a blank word-processing document and, starting at the upper left corner, simply "thinking through writing," writing sentence after sentence about whatever you're thinking as quickly as you're thinking it, in a stream-of-consciousness manner. Your goal is to get as much of your thinking down as you can.

We find free-writing one of the best ways to help focus thoughts. Sometimes we might write for a good quarter- or half-page, but, amazingly, we always eventually get to a sentence or two that seems to capture exactly where we were headed—in this case, our purpose for writing a particular letter.

Example of a free-writing session:

> *Okay, I'm having a hard time getting clear about why I'm writing to X company. I know I'm ticked at how that rep treated me on the phone, and you know this isn't the first time I've gotten that treatment from this company. Boy, I'd love to get that wealthy*

> *president on the phone! Okay…okay, where am I going with this?*
> *I want something done this time. I don't owe them anything! And I*
> *resent having to go through this month after month because their*
> *"system" screws up! I'm tired of talking to one person after*
> *another—repeating my story time after time—and no one…some*
> *guarantee. That's what I want: one person handling my account and*
> *getting rid of these fees once and for all!! And if I don't get this, I'll*
> *take my business elsewhere…*

Write without concern for spelling, punctuation, or even well-structured sentences. Just write!

The above free-writing resulted in this purpose statement:

> *The purpose of this letter is to persuade the president of X company*
> *to make sure I'm no longer charged late fees when my payments*
> *aren't late and to notify her that if some **one** person doesn't call me*
> *back within the next two weeks to rectify this situation, I'll take my*
> *business to Y company.*

Analyze your audience

The strongest communications are audience-focused. Think of the last party you attended, at which you felt stuck listening to the long-winded bore who seemed oblivious of the fact you had no interest whatsoever in what he was saying. Was he communicating effectively with you?

And what about you? Would you communicate the same way with an attorney as you would your son's second-grade teacher? Would a surgeon you met once and your neighborhood grocery read a letter from you the same way? Would they be looking for the same kinds of things in that communication?

Truly communicating (in a letter or in other ways) requires focusing in a bit on to whom you're writing.

Take the time to analyze each important reader in your audience. What do you know about him or her:

- How does this person typically communicate: With facts? With feelings?

- How much does he know about the topic?

- Is she interested in the topic? Will she care about what you have to say?

- How will your message affect him?

- Might she have resistance to your message? Will it kick up any concerns?

- What, if anything, will he expect or need to find in this communication?

One way to help you focus more fully on the specific needs and interests of the recipient of your letter is to quickly list all the characteristics you can think of to describe him or her. The more specific you can get with this list, the better directed your communication will be.

What if you don't know the person you're writing to? You could just skip this step and assume you're writing to the Average Joe. But if your goal is to write a better letter—a letter more likely to get results—take the time to analyze your audience, even if all you can do is take good educated guesses about the person you assume will read your letter.

Sometimes a profession or position will offer some hints. Most people in highly technical positions, for instance, value facts, figures, accuracy, and lots of objective information in their communications; these individuals typically mistrust letters that come across as too emotional or too much like a sales spiel. People in hard-driving, decision-making roles typically value concise, direct communication and the bottom line; you'll want to get to your point quickly and go light on the details. Individuals in support roles, such as a secretary or departmental assistant, tend to value long-term relationships, stability, and clear direction in their communications; to take dramatic action on your behalf, they'll first need to trust you, then they'll want clear directions. Finally, those in sales, advertising, or other promotional roles tend to highly value others' opinions and to maintain a host of interests simultaneously; you'll need to do something a little unique to get and keep their focus on your concerns.

Brainstorm your ideas on the subject

If you've ever finished a long letter only to realize you might have approached it more effectively a different way, you know the value of brainstorming your ideas ahead of time. Getting your ideas out in front of you first can help you better work with those ideas to develop a more strategic approach to what you're writing.

Brainstorming on paper (or computer) is similar to brainstorming with a group. The goal is the same: to list as many ideas on a topic as quickly as you can. The only way most people can do this is to accept, without judging its merits, any idea. If it comes into your head, write it down. And write it down in any form it comes—a word, a phrase, or perhaps a sentence. Just try to keep it in the form of a list rather than a paragraph.

And even seemingly irrelevant ideas should go down. If you lose your focus and start thinking about ideas completely unrelated to this letter, write them down anyway! Why? The minute you begin to allow judgmental comments to critique your thoughts—comments such as "This doesn't relate" or "This is a stupid idea"— you're crippling your own creative process. Simply get all the ideas you can in front of you in list form. You'll evaluate the merit of these ideas later.

To brainstorm, follow these simple steps:

1. Find a quiet space, free of distractions.

2. Set a timer for 3 to 5 minutes. (Three if you feel you have little to say; five if you have a lot to say.)

3. Start your timer.

4. Write as quickly as you can—without stopping—until your time is up.

Why write quickly? Experts say we can think at a rate of about 500 words per minute. But we can write down only about 30 words a minute, even fewer if we're critiquing our thoughts and trying to find just the right words. Write just as the thoughts occur to you, even if the words aren't the perfect ones or spelled correctly. Correctness is the least of your concerns. Don't stop to make corrections. This can be especially tempting if you're brainstorming on computer. Avoid the urge to correct *anything*! Instead, see your goal as documenting every thought in your head! If you're brainstorming well, your hand will probably be tired at the 3- or 5-minute mark!

Why write without pausing? You may periodically have the urge to pause as you search for the next thought. Unfortunately, pauses give your brain just enough time to second-guess or analyze your thoughts. Keep writing down your thoughts nonstop, and this analysis is less likely to happen. But keeping the writing going can be challenging. One trick to keep yourself writing is this: Whenever you notice that you're pausing, keep your pen moving or your fingers typing by simply repeating the very last word you wrote down. Write it down over and over, if needed, until the next thought comes. With practice, you'll find it easy to write quickly and nonstop for the entire time you've set.

Here's a final tip on brainstorming: Keep writing until your predetermined time is up. Very often some of our best ideas come to us in the last minute or so of brainstorming. We're not sure why this happens, but our brains seem to need a chance to clear away the junk and so-so ideas before it can reveal some real gems. Students and others who have used this technique report having the same experience. So keep writing. After you've tried this with a letter or two, you may to decide to slightly increase or decrease your time: Base this decision on how much time you seem to need so you feel "finished."

Group like ideas

Quickly group ideas that seem to naturally fit together. The trick here is to "think from your gut." Think in terms of which ideas might belong in the same paragraph or group of paragraphs. The process you use to group like ideas is up to you. With the computer's word-processing program, you can apply shading or background color to words or phrases in order to identify different groups of ideas. On paper, you might use different colored highlighters to identify groups of ideas. You can also draw arrows between ideas that go together, draw or insert circles or boxes around groups of like ideas, or use some system to categorize each idea, such as a numbering or lettering system (this goes with Idea A; this with Idea B; and so on).

Order your groups

Next, order your groups of like ideas into a "living outline." Your goal here is to establish a first-impulse order only. Review your entire list of groups of ideas and quickly throw your groups into a rough order. You can do this by cutting and pasting your text on screen or rewriting your ideas in order on paper. (Your letter might start with group C ideas, then go to group A ideas, and so forth.) Remember, you can always change your mind later, as you draft, if a better order occurs to you. Consider this an initial blueprint—just a way to begin the writing.

Drafting your letter

Most people spend entirely too much time drafting a letter, especially when it's a more challenging letter to write. When you begin the draft of your letter, if you struggle to get rolling; find yourself grueling over almost every word, making sure to say precisely what you mean, exactly as you mean to say it, without oversimplifying or offending; feel that the writing goes extremely slowly; or find you're crossing off a good number of the words you first wrote down, again, check how you're approaching it. There is an easier way!

Drafting should take very little time and feel very much like brainstorming. If you've completed the advanced-thinking steps we've just described, drafting requires simply taking your groups of ideas, in basically the order you set out in your blueprint, and *quickly* drafting a paragraph or so on each. Your goal is to write in rough—really rough—paragraphs. Try not to cross out or delete as you go. Instead, continue to "think from your gut." We find it helpful, again, to think in terms of "just getting it down." Trust that you'll spend time editing later. Editing, or really polishing up your thinking, is always easier when you've got *something* to work with. Draft now. Edit later. Unless, of course, you enjoy the more time-consuming and painful alternative. Then try doing both at the same time.

Part of the beauty of this process is that you can start writing from anywhere on the blueprint. Many people find the first paragraph of a letter the most difficult to write. Who says you have to start at the beginning of your blueprint? Jump in somewhere easy first. Go back and write the first paragraph later, when it might come more easily anyway.

Editing your letter

Always take time to edit a first draft. If you've drafted your letter using the process we've described, your draft should be rough! But the thoughts are basically there now, so you'll have an easier time going back over it critically to really polish up your thinking.

Edit your letter only after you've given your draft "time to cool." Get some distance from it—ideally 24 hours. If you can afford to wait, you'll find things that you want to change more quickly. What should you focus on as you edit your letter? Editing, to us, involves three fundamental goals: clarifying, strengthening, and condensing your message. For tips on how to edit and finally proofread your letter, refer to Debra Hart May's book *Proofreading Plain & Simple* (published by Career Press).

CHAPTER 4

Entice Your Reader to Read—From Beginning to End

What makes for an effective personal business or social letter, a letter people are likely to respond to and perhaps even appreciate reading? To answer that question, think about what you like or dislike about the letters you receive in your home.

- Do they move you to read them?

- Do they express the business at hand quickly and clearly?

- Do they make the information you expect or need from them easy to find?

- Do they use language you find interesting, meaningful, and easy to understand?

- Do they entice you to keep reading?

- Are you likely to take the action they request?

These are some fundamental aspects of an effective letter (as well as effective communication in general). Certainly, not all letters you receive in your home pass muster on these few basic points. Most that come into our homes don't! But the fact that you're reading this book means your letters will be a cut above the mediocre and even poor letters many people use to attempt to communicate.

6 basic purposes for writing a letter

Most every letter you'll ever write, whether business or social in nature, hopes to accomplish one of six basic purposes. Identify the type of letter you're writing by its purpose, and you'll be better able to both maintain your letter's focus and chose the letter template or recommended strategy that will best get the job done!

Some letters can attempt more than one purpose at a time, but the most effective letters ideally attempt one, and no more than two, of these basic purposes in any single letter. Letters that try to accomplish more than this typically do not read like thoughtful, well-developed messages, but instead like grocery lists—snatches of loosely related items, none of which is described with enough detail to be truly helpful to anyone but the one who wrote the list!

How you structure your letter should be guided by the overriding, or primary, purpose you want the letter to accomplish. Here are those six basic purposes:

1. To request information or routine action.

From "Please repair my watch under warranty" to "Send me an application" to "Please provide guidelines for starting a recycling program in my neighborhood," these letters are typically less emotionally-charged and deal with relatively straight-forward requests.

2. To persuade someone to take action.

This action can be anything from "Consider me for a position" to "Please resolve my complaint." These letters address more than routine requests and are the ones to which you might suspect some resistance from the reader.

3. To demand action.

These letters are appropriate after a kinder request or two, by phone, e-mail, or previous letters, didn't do the job. Firmly handling an awkward situation without alienating those with the power to correct it is generally the goal of a letter demanding action.

4. To provide information or describe an event.

Often these letters respond to a request someone has made of you, such as "Here is the transcript you requested," but they may also describe your independent action, such as "I resign as committee chair." If your purpose is merely to provide information, you expect no further action.

5. To acknowledge information or an event.

Holiday greetings fall into this category, as do recognition, congratulation, and thank-you letters. A letter merely acknowledging receipt of some message, information, or product also serves this purpose.

6. To convey bad news or decline a request.

Delivering bad news in a letter is challenging. If your goal is to maintain some form of relationship with the letter's recipient, you must "soften" the bad news—in other words, deliver it more slowly and with tact and kindness. Saying no, when someone has made a request you must decline, also requires graceful handling and a unique approach.

In Chapter 7 and accompanying the sample letters and e-mails throughout the book, you'll find templates and recommended strategies for approaching these six different types of letters. These templates will work for any letter-writing situation with a purpose, from letters more social in nature to those that strive to accomplish some form of "business" (in other words, letters that strive to get something specific done), whether with a government entity, a corporation, a nonprofit or civic group, a friend, or a family member.

Characteristics of a good business-oriented letter

Regardless of your letter's purpose, good communication is good communication. Following are characteristics of letters we'd take the time to read in their entirety—and probably respond to quickly.

A letter begins well if it...

☞ **Looks easy to read.**

This means, fundamentally, short paragraphs. When we glance at the first page, the paragraphs have to appear short (ideally, no more than six or eight lines—and that's *lines*, not *sentences*). Short paragraphs suggest a quick read. We think, "Good. I won't have to set this aside right now (chances are, to get lost in some pile somewhere) so I can dig it back out later and read it when I have more time," which may never happen.

Another way to make a letter look easier to read is to use bulleted or numbered lists whenever possible. Consider the following two ways to display the same information:

1. Our new curbside recycling program will accept all aluminum and bi-metal cans (crush these to save space) and steel food cans with labels removed. It will also accept glass containers (green, brown, or clear), with lids discarded, and plastic containers labeled #1 or #2. Newspapers will also be accepted, but these must be bundled and kept dry for pick up.

2. Our new curbside recycling program will accept:

   • Aluminum and bimetal cans (crushed to save space).

   • Steel food cans (labels removed).

   • Glass containers (green, brown, or clear, without lids).

   • Plastic containers (labeled #1 or #2).

   • Newspapers (bundled and kept dry).

☞ **Seems easy to understand.**

The sentences and words used should make the message easy to understand. Short sentences (averaging no more than 10 to 20 words) and common everyday language help us comprehend the message quickly. Don't use expressions such as "articulate" when you mean "say" or "subsequently" when you mean "after." Consider this: The general public reads at only about a fourth-grade reading level.

Even if your particular reader has stronger reading skills, reading strings of long, obscure words takes a lot of work! For even the most highly educated, common language communicates most effectively.

☞ Speaks to the reader personally.

Letters communicate person to person. We're alienated by letters that begin with stilted, impersonal "business speak." Expressions such as "per your request," "with regard to the above-referenced," or "enclosed herewith" sound less than human, somehow, and seem to indicate an indifference to the reader as an individual.

Good writing demonstrates attention to what the reader needs to get from the letter. Certainly, the writer of any letter attempts to get his or her message across, but, for the reader to accept that message, it must be delivered in a way that expresses empathy for the reader's perspective. One way to build empathy into your writing is to use a lot more "you" language than "I" or "we" language. Does your writing demonstrate empathy? If so, it uses second person (expressing a "you" perspective) more often than first person (expressing an "I" or "we" perspective).

The best way to demonstrate this point is to show you an example that expresses little empathy. Imagine you received the following letter from your bank:

Dear _____:

At XYZ Bank, providing superior service to our customers is our first goal. We are a customer-oriented company that seeks to attract loyal clients by creating products that meet their needs. In this vein, we are introducing several new products we feel are sure to meet our valued customers' ever-changing banking needs....

The letter misses the mark when it comes to expressing empathy. Consider the difference that more "you" than "we" language can make, in the following example:

Dear _____:

Serving you, our customer, is XYZ Bank's first goal. Your needs are important to us, and to keep you with us as a customer, we must offer you products that meet your changing needs. In this vein, you should know about these new products....

Which letter would appeal more to you? Which version seems less focused on XYZ Bank's interests and more focused on yours?

Notice that writing with empathy doesn't mean eliminating every first-person reference. What the second example attempts to do, however, is provide a balance, using at least as many empathy-expressing "you" references as writer-focused "we" references.

☞ Treats the reader with courtesy.

"You" language doesn't work, however, when it's used to tell the reader what to do or what he or she did wrong. Nothing forces the hair on the back of our necks to stand up more quickly than someone saying "you must," "you should have," or "you should not have." If your reader needs direction, direct him or her intelligently and with courtesy.

By *intelligently*, we mean keep your reader in mind. Don't give your reader obvious direction or advice such as "Be sure to attach proper postage next time." And when your reader might disagree with your direction, show him or her why doing things your way is in his or her best interest:

- ▱ "To help you avoid any further difficulties..."

- ▱ "To help you get the response you're looking for..."

- ▱ "To help our block become eligible for Crime Watch..."

By *courteously*, we mean use courteous words (*please* and *thank you* continue to work wonders!) and a courteous tone. *Never* tell a reader he or she has to do something. Simply say:

- ▱ "Please complete this questionnaire..."

- ▱ "Would you consider hosting a Crime Watch meeting?"

◿ **Reveals immediately what it's about *and how it affects the reader personally.***

Get to the point. We typically won't read a letter that doesn't get to the point immediately. As we begin to read a letter, we think, "What's the point here, and what do you want from me?" If the writer hasn't answered these questions in the first couple of sentences, we may scan another line or two, but we'll rarely ever read the thing word for word. Most likely, we'll stop reading altogether.

Where do you typically get to the point? Few people feel they have time to waste when reading a business-oriented letter. Do you? (Do you read your junk mail?) Most readers become unmotivated to continue very quickly—within a document's first sentence or two—if the document doesn't immediately spell out not only what the document is about, but *how it involves them*.

Think of this as the "So what?" factor. After reading your letter's first or second sentence, could your intended reader possibly respond, "So what?"

Consider this complaint letter to a furniture store:

Dear Customer Service Manager:

I was assured last week that the bookshelves we ordered from your store six weeks ago would be delivered to our home this past weekend. Your representative (I believe his name was Roy) told my husband last week that the bookshelves were on the delivery schedule, and he asked us to make sure someone would be home this past Saturday to receive the delivery. But no one arrived all day with our bookshelves. (We waited until around 8 p.m. and made several phone calls; repeatedly someone at your store told us they were on the way.)

This entire situation would not be so upsetting were it not for the fact that we were originally told we'd receive the bookshelves in two weeks, not six! When they didn't arrive as promised the first time, we eventually learned (from someone named Sharon) that a problem with your distributor forced you to delay delivery. I accepted the new delivery date, but just how much longer...

If you were this customer service manager, probably a very busy person, how would you respond to this letter (which only begins to get to the point at the end of this passage)? Sure, this person's job is to help you, and he or she will probably be forced to read—or have someone else read—this letter word for word to do so. But why didn't the writer get this manager on her side from the beginning? Consider the difference when a letter like this gets right to the point:

Dear Customer Service Manager:

Please help me get the bookshelves I ordered six weeks ago from your store but never received! I've experienced a long series of mishaps with your store regarding these bookshelves, and I'm looking to you to correct this as soon as possible.

The second version tells the manager immediately why this customer is writing, and what she wants that manager to do about her dilemma.

The details of what specifically happened may still be important for the manager to know (it may help the manager solve this customer's problem), but this information belongs in the middle of this letter, not the beginning. Again, think of yourself as the manager. Wouldn't you be more interested in reading the details of the situation after you know what the basic situation is and that it's relevant to you? (Maybe some other department manager should be handling the whole situation!)

Should writers always get right to the point? If you have read Chapter 3, you're probably expecting a resounding *Yes!* Well, here's our answer: *Yes, almost all the time.* And here's why. In a very small number of situations, getting right to the point may so disappoint, anger, or turn off your reader that he or she may not continue reading. Think of a time you received bad news, especially on paper. "We have offered the job to another applicant." "Your Letter to the Editor arrived too late for publication." A letter that starts with such a line would be nothing short of painful to continue reading.

Avoid stating your point immediately in two types of situations:

- Letters whose primary purpose is conveying bad news.

- Letters whose primary purpose is attempting to persuade—when the proposal will likely come as a surprise to its *reader*.

Let's say you rent an apartment, and you decide to write a letter to your landlord to persuade him or her to take care of some maintenance problem. Your landlord might expect this type of letter (or at least not be surprised at what you propose). So go ahead and get right to the point.

On the other hand, let's say you write to your landlord with some off-the-wall proposal ("Hey, I know some great property for sale; want to partner with me...?") Chances are, your landlord will be surprised by such a unique proposal. To avoid a quick turn-down, delay getting to your point. Instead, start with information that might otherwise come in the letter's middle section—rationale for partnering with you on this deal.

Note: In many, if not most, persuasive letters, the reader expects the proposal, at least in a general way. When this is the case, your best approach is, again, to get right to the point. Don't wait. We'll talk more about this later when we address templates for persuasive letters in Chapter 7.

The middle of a letter works well when it...

☞ **Continues to respect the reader's needs and perspective.**

To stay interested in a letter, we need to continue to have our needs met. We need to receive information in an order we expect and that is most useful to us. Again, if the letter ever begins to seem irrelevant to us, we'll start scanning it or put it down.

If the letter is intended to be persuasive or deals with a controversial topic, a reader will be on the lookout for vague or less-than-complete information. Present your point with some attention to the reader's perspective and he or she will probably keep reading, even if you give your perspective more weight.

Different readers are persuaded to see your point of view in different ways. Here, again, is where knowing something about your reader can really pay off. Your reader will most likely be persuaded in one of four ways:

1. Some look for facts, details, or objective proof.

2. Some look for a creative or expressive appeal.

3. Some look for a bottom-line, decisive approach.

4. Some look for a reassuring, low-risk appeal.

Please note that condescending or angry letters rarely ever persuade. They more typically put people off, make them angry, and make their cooperation a lot less likely. *Never write a letter in anger.* Letters are more permanent than phone calls. They tend to leave a longer lasting impression, and they can end relationships.

☞ **Is easy to follow from thought to thought.**

Each paragraph should cover one main idea that is clearly expressed in that paragraph's first line or two. Don't make someone read an entire paragraph before he or she finds out what that paragraph's main idea is; give it to the reader right away. A reader should even be able to scan first sentences of paragraphs to get the gist of what's in each paragraph. (These first sentences are called *topic sentences*.)

Then, to help keep a reader focused on each paragraph's main idea, the paragraph should support, or more fully explain, only that idea. It might go into a little more detail to further explain what you mean, or qualify your point by specifying that your point holds true in some circumstances but not in others. It may also provide examples, further arguments, or "evidence" to prove the paragraph's point.

Both your sentences and paragraphs should come in an order that makes the most sense to the reader. Don't toss the reader from one thought to another that, from the reader's perspective, appear unrelated. One very specific way to help weave a logical flow between your sentences and paragraphs is to use transitional expressions between them (for example, words such as "then" in the previous paragraph and "finally," in the next).

Finally, the grammar and punctuation should be correct. Mistakes in the "mechanics" of the language make comprehension difficult—and leave a poor impression of the author.

✍ Makes the information the reader needs most easy to find.

We'll make one more plug here for bulleted lists, numbered lists, and other scanable ways of displaying information. If your reader will need to refer back to a date, an account number, an address—whatever it is—put a box around it, or surround it with white space (by double spacing above and below the information and sometimes indenting from both side margins). Help your reader find the information she needs!

✍ Expresses information concisely.

Everyone is too busy to read even a few extra words. Say what you have to say as concisely, directly, and simply as possible. Leave out information that you find interesting but that your reader won't need. Cut every word that doesn't add meaning to a sentence. And avoid cliché business language such as "with regard to the matter of," and eliminate unnecessary sentence warm-ups, such as "It is important that..." and "There are many reasons why...." Write as you would speak to the recipient of your letter.

Don't say:

> I am writing to inform you that there are several reasons why it is very important that alternate action be taken with regard to the above-mentioned matter due to the fact that a decision was made with which disagreement could be expressed.

Say:

> Please reverse this decision; I disagree with it.

A letter ends well if it...

✍ Gives contact information.

Even the best letter you can write may leave a question in the reader's mind that you didn't anticipate. Because letter-writing is essentially one-way communication, make responding to your letter easy: Give a phone number (or other contact number or e-mail address) so the reader can get *all* the necessary information quickly and easily:

> "If you have questions about this year's annual camping outing, please call me at…."

☛ Ends with sincerity, not cliché.

Except in cases when a very professional and impersonal tone is appropriate, don't use boring, stale expressions that can make a letter seem like a business form letter rather than a sincere letter from a human being. Notice in the example above that we added the words "about this year's annual camping outing" to the otherwise cliché business expression, "If you have questions, please call."

Probably the most common of these cliché expressions is, "Please don't hesitate to call." ("Gee, I hadn't thought about hesitating, but now that you mention it….") Even the expression "Feel free to call" has become tired and overused, and some people find it condescending ("Gee, thanks for giving me permission….").

Even worse, don't presume the reader will do what you want because you've thanked him or her "in advance." This is another cliché business expression that many people find presumptive ("How can you thank me? I haven't done it yet.") or dismissive ("Sure, thank me ahead of time to get this whole situation out of your hair.").

☛ Prompts the reader to act.

Even though the beginning of the letter told the reader why you're writing and what, specifically, you want from him or her, consider this: Research has shown that readers are most likely to remember the very last thing they read! So use your letter's very last line to restate the action you're expecting your reader to take.

☛ Ends with courtesy.

Again, because readers probably remember the last impression they get from a letter, make sure you end your letter graciously. Never lose sight of the fact that the decision to cooperate—or not—is ultimately the reader's! Convey your request as a request, not a demand:

> 📝 "Please consider contributing today."

> 📝 "I would appreciate a prompt response."

Is giving a deadline appropriate? If a prompt response is important to you and seems reasonable to request, yes, setting a response deadline is completely appropriate. Make sure your date is realistic (consider mail time and so on), and state the deadline specifically and tactfully. Exact dates stick in peoples' minds better than expressions such as "Please respond within 10 days of receiving this letter." And the best method we know to add tact to a deadline is to justify the reason for it with a brief phrase:

> 📝 "To help us plan for this event, please RSVP by January 5."

> 📝 "To make sure we locate as many of our classmates as possible, please call Joan or me by September 15."

The best phrases justify a reason the recipient of the letter will find beneficial:

☞ "To help me get this payment to you quickly, please respond to these questions by March 20."

☞ "To save us both time during this busy time of year, please call me with your order by November 25."

The editor's checklist

Every well-written letter, memo, fax, or e-mail message should "EMCEE" the communication:

Entice your reader.

Meet your reader's needs.

Communicate your message clearly.

Express your thoughts concisely.

End memorably.

The checklist that follows summarizes what we consider key aspects of any good letter. It will...

Entice your reader to read if it:

❑ States its purpose clearly, and in most cases, immediately.

❑ States up front *action you're wanting from the reader.*

❑ Makes its purpose relevant to the reader—states *why* he or she should read it.

❑ Demonstrates audience-focus by using more "you" than "we" language.

❑ Uses language most appropriate for the reader.

❑ Avoids unnecessary use of impersonal business clichés, such as "per your request," "enclosed please find," "with regard to the above matter," "received this date," and so on.

❑ Sets a tone likely to get the intended response.

Meet your reader's needs if it:

❑ Presents information in "scanable" ways (for example, short paragraphs or bulleted lists).

❑ Gives information in the order the reader would want it.

❑ Includes as much information as the reader would want or need.

Communicate your message clearly if it:

❏ Uses correct grammar and punctuation.

❏ Contains unified paragraphs (one main thought per paragraph).

❏ Starts its paragraphs with topic sentences.

❏ Helps thoughts flow logically with ample (but varied) transitional expressions.

Express your thoughts concisely if it:

❏ Avoids "it" and "there" sentence warm-ups ("It is important that…"; "There are many reasons why….").

❏ Avoids empty expressions such as "I am writing to inform you," "I am requesting," or "The purpose of this letter is to…."

❏ Avoids wordy, lofty-sounding expressions such as "at this point in time" ("now"), "due to the fact that" ("because"), and "in the event that" ("if").

❏ Uses active versus passive voice ("He solved the problem" versus "The problem was solved"), except in situations calling for tact.

❏ Uses strong verbs, not noun phrases ("decided" versus "made a decision").

❏ Reduces ("that" or "which") clauses to phrases and reduces phrases to single words.

End memorably if it:

❏ Offers contact information for further communication.

❏ Restates the point or needed action with its last line.

❏ Ends with courtesy.

For more information on these and other grammar concepts, check out *The Gregg Reference Manual* by William A. Sabin (published by Glencoe/McGraw-Hill); for practice exercises to improve your grammar skills, see *Better Grammar in 30 Minutes a Day* by Constance Immel and Florence Sacks (published by Career Press).

CHAPTER 5

The Parts of a Letter

The parts of a letter are standard and have remained so for centuries. Out of convenience to your reader, include the parts they expect. However, you may deviate from the norm when doing so would be even more helpful to your reader. For instance, you might include your telephone number or e-mail address in a line added to your letter's heading; someone looking for this information will probably look for it there first.

Whether you're writing a business-oriented letter or a letter written strictly for social purposes, the parts of your letter are essentially the same. Even e-mails written for business and nonsocial purposes should contain the same parts. Social letters and e-mails tend to omit a few parts always included in business letters, as we will outline below. How you format your letter (where you place these individual parts on the page) also depends on whether its focus is business or social. And even then you have some options. Chapter 6 covers standard letter and envelope formats.

Another thing to realize is that you can probably take advantage of the letter-composing tool that most word-processing programs now have. Such features allow you to select a template for a particular kind of letter—business, casual, thank-you, complaint, and so on. Then the program walks you through each part of the letter, allowing you to plug in the appropriate information piece by piece. The computer then generates your letter for you, and then you can open it and make adjustments. The only problem with such letter tools is that they may ask you to fill in fields that are not necessary or appropriate for your unique writing situation, which is why you need this book!

Heading or stationery letterhead

Letters, whether business or social in nature, typically start with some indication of who's sending the letter. Only the most informal of social letters omit the heading. Of course, some preprinted stationery already provides this information.

41

In workplace e-mail, you could insert a company logo if you're sending your e-mail to an outside contact; otherwise, for internal workplace e-mails, you will need nothing more than your signature (see the section on signatures on page 45).

The heading may include the sender's name (considered optional in social letters as you will sign the letter) and a full address. Typically, this address is fully spelled out, including the state name (versus using the two-letter state abbreviation) in a personal letter, whether business or socially oriented.

Date

This is the month, day, and year you write the letter. All letters you write should include a date, for the letter recipient's information and—if you keep a copy—your own future reference.

To avoid any confusion, always spell out the name of the month, and use the standard order of month, day, and year, such as "December 5, 2004."

Reference line

Business-oriented letters may include a single reference line identifying an account, customer, or file number:

Reference: Customer Number 568-399049

Including this information can help a customer service representative, for instance, to quickly find the information he or she needs to help you.

Social letters do not include reference lines. In e-mail, your reference line should be typed into the "Subject:" field of your message.

Mail or confidential notation

Business-oriented letters may also include a notation indicating any special handling your letter should receive:

CERTIFIED MAIL   *or*   CONFIDENTIAL

"Confidential" indicates that no one but the addressee should read this letter. The envelope, too, should indicate that a letter is confidential. (See Chapter 6 for tips on addressing an envelope.) For emphasis, write these notations either in all capital letters or underlined with initial capitals: Certified Mail.

Social letters typically do not include these notations. Also, remember that e-mail is not the right forum for confidential disclosures.

Inside address

This is the recipient's full name and address. Business-oriented personal letters should always include this information on the letter itself, because the business or organization to which you send your letter may separate it from its envelope. Include the recipient's name, if you know it, that person's job title and/or department name, organization name, and address (again fully spelled out, including the state name). If you don't have a recipient's name or you're not sure how to handle the *Mr.*, *Mrs.*, *Miss*, or *Ms.*, you have some options. (See Chapter 6.)

Social letters typically omit the inside address.

Attention line

Attention lines are tools to help ensure that your business-oriented letter is acted upon. Included also on the envelope, an attention line can be used in a couple of ways:

- "Attention" appearing before someone's name on the first line of the inside address (or the envelope's address) indicates that this person should handle your letter:

    Attention: Charles Kidd, Customer Service Representative
    ABC Electronics
    459 Electronics Way
    Cincinnati, OH zip+4

- An attention line appearing after an inside address that includes an individual's name indicates that if the recipient is not available, this second person should receive your letter. If you don't have a name, then a position or department name will also ensure that the letter gets to the right place:

    Charles Kidd, Customer Service Representative
    ABC Electronics
    459 Electronics Way
    Cincinnati, OH zip+4
    Attention: Customer Service Manager

Social letters do not include attention lines.

Salutation

This is the greeting of either a business or social letter, typically beginning with the word "Dear." Use this standard greeting unless your purpose is very informal. Informal salutations can start directly with the recipient's first name ("Mark,") or be as casual as a "Hi!"

Should you use your recipient's first name or use a surname with a courtesy title (Mr., Mrs., Miss, or Ms.)? In a social letter, base this decision on your relationship with that person. How would you speak to him or her on the telephone? More business-oriented letters offer many creative options especially useful when you're not sure of your recipient's gender (as with a "Terry" or a "Jamie") or you're not sure if she is a Mrs., Miss, or Ms. (See Chapter 6.)

Social salutations end with a comma; business salutations typically end with a colon, but also may end with a comma for a more casual business approach. You may opt for a comma, for instance, if you use the recipient's first name in the salutation.

Business Salutations:	**Social Salutations:**
Dear Mr. Clark:	Dear Mr. Tomms,
Dear John Clark:	Dear Joe,
Dear John,	Joe,

Subject line

A subject line is optional in business-oriented letters except for the atypical simplified letter business format, which, because it omits the salutation, requires this brief summary of the letter's purpose to help ensure the letter gets into the right hands. Social letters do not use subject lines.

For e-mails, use the "Subject:" field of your message for your subject line if you haven't already used it as a field for a reference number or reference information (see "Reference line" on page 42).

Body of the letter

The body of the letter includes the main text of the letter. Lines of text within the body are generally single-spaced with double spacing between paragraphs. Depending on the letter format you choose, the first line of each new paragraph may also be indented. (See letter and envelope formats in Chapter 7.)

Complimentary close

The complimentary close is the polite sign-off of either a business or social letter, generally composed of just a word or two. The close you choose indicates the level of formality or intimacy you wish to express. Certain closes are generally more appropriate for business use, others, for social use. But there are no hard-and-fast rules. A business-oriented letter addressed to someone you know well, for instance, might use a close more typically used for social purposes.

With closes of more than one word, capitalize only the first word. Complimentary closes always end with a comma.

Appropriate Business Closes:

Sincerely,	Regards,
Sincerely yours,	Kind regards,
Respectfully,	Yours truly,
Cordially,	

Appropriate Social Closes:

Best wishes,	Affectionately,
All the best,	Your friend,
Very truly yours,	As ever,
Warmly,	Always,
Fondly,	With love,
Faithfully,	Love,

Signature

All letters, whether business or social in nature, require a signature. Business-oriented letters, if they're typed, generally also include the writer's full name typed on a line beneath the signature. A hand-written business letter typically does not include an additional signature line.

For a more casual touch, sign using the form of your name you want the letter's recipient to use. If, for instance, your formal name is "Albert Jones," but you go by "Al," you might sign "Al" but print or type "Albert Jones" below your signature. If appropriate, your business-oriented letter might also include your title, printed or typed in the line below your printed full name. Social letters include only the signature.

(A "signature" in e-mail means something entirely different. Refer to page 18 in Chapter 2 for details.)

Additional notations

Additional notations communicate, often in a type of code, administrative details about your letter. These are more typically used for business-oriented letters, but on occasion you might find them useful for social letters. Use notations at the end of your letter to:

☞ Indicate that something is enclosed with the letter:

Enclosure or Enc.

Enclosures or Encs.

Enclosure: check

Check enclosed

☞ Indicate that something is attached to the letter (actually affixed to the letter, as with a paper clip or staple):

Attachment

Attachments

Attached: copy of receipt

Copy of receipt attached

✉ Indicate that something else has been sent:

Under separate cover: photographs

Photos coming under separate cover.

✉ Inform that others are also receiving copies of this letter:

Copy: Sue Taylor

Copies: Sue Taylor   or   *Copies to: Sue Taylor*
           Rob Wallis   *Rob Wallis*

c: Sue Taylor   or   *cc: Sue Taylor*

c: Sue Taylor   or   *cc: Sue Taylor*
   Rob Wallis   *Rob Wallis*

✉ Request a response:

RSVP (French for "Respond, if you please.")

Please respond by _____. (Insert appropriate date.)

Regrets only. (Respond only if you're not coming.)

Postscript

Postscripts are brief comments tacked on at the end of typically social letters, but they may be included in business-oriented letters as well. In social letters, they include information that would be construed as irrelevant to the main thrust of the letter. In social letters, postscripts usually begin with "P.S."; business postscripts may or may not begin with "P.S."

Postscripts are often used as final persuasive pitches in business letters. If you use a postscript in a business-oriented letter, make sure the information it contains is appropriate as a postscript—don't use a postscript simply to make up for poor planning. If you do, your efforts may appear less than business-like to the recipient of your letter.

For tips on handling issues related to formatting—where these parts of a letter should appear on the page—see Chapter 7.

CHAPTER 6

Forms of Address

Using the appropriate form of address both expresses respect for the recipient of your letter and, in a business-oriented letter, demonstrates your professionalism. This holds true in electronic mail as well.

Each example on the following pages lists the form of address to appear in the inside address, as well as on the envelope, followed by the form of address for the salutation.

The examples are divided into the following categories:

- Social titles.
- Professional titles.
- Corporate titles.
- State and local government titles.
- U.S. government titles.
- U.S., state, and local court titles.
- Diplomatic titles.
- Military titles.
- Religious titles.
- College and university titles.

Social titles

Men

When your recipient has one, use professional titles or degree designations, not social titles:

Address:　Dr. John Smith　　*or*　　John Smith, Ph.D.
Salutation: Dear Dr. Smith:

In the absence of a professional title, you have the option to use a social title or use the person's first and last name (without a title) in the inside address. Using a social title lends an air of formality. The alternative of using just a first and last name has become quite acceptable in most instances.

Address: Mr. John Smith   *or*   John Smith
Salutation: Dear Mr. Smith: *or*   Dear John Smith:

If you have a close relationship with the recipient, another option for the salutation (only) is to use just the first name. When using a first name, use either a colon or a comma to end the salutation.

Salutation: Dear John: *or*   Dear John,

When a man has a *Jr.*, *Sr.*, or Roman numeral after his name, do not repeat these in the salutation.

Address: Mr. John Smith III   *or*   John Smith III
Salutation: Dear Mr. Smith: *or*   Dear John Smith:

Address: Mr. John Smith, Jr.   *or*   John Smith, Jr.
Salutation: Dear Mr. Smith: *or*   Dear John Smith:

When addressing several men, avoid the formal *Messrs.* (French for *Misters*) except in extremely formal or legal correspondence. Instead, list each man's name in both the inside address and the salutation. When all recipients are men, *Gentlemen* is also acceptable although somewhat formal.

Address: Mr. John Smith   John Smith
              Mr. Tom Jones   *or* Tom Jones
            · ·Mr. Joe Thomas   Joe Thomas
Salutation: Dear Mr. Smith, Mr. Jones, and Mr. Thomas:
                              or
              Dear John Smith, Tom Jones, and Joe Thomas:
                              or
              Dear John, Tom, and Joe: (if close relationship)

Women

In the absence of a professional title, use a social title or use the person's first and last name (without a title) in the inside address.

Address: Mrs. Jane Smith   *or*   Jane Smith
Salutation: Dear Mrs. Smith: *or*   Dear Jane Smith:

If you have a close relationship with the recipient, you may opt to use just a first name (in the salutation only). When using a first name, use either a colon or a comma to end the salutation.

Salutation: Dear Jane: *or*   Dear Jane,

Mrs., Ms., Miss? The only completely safe bet when using a woman's social title is to know and use her preference. Using a first and last name without a social title has become widely acceptable, in fact, simply because determining the correct title can be such a challenge.

If you wish to use a social title and don't know a woman's marital status, *Ms.* has become widely used as a generic title for all three. (Although be aware that some women really prefer *Miss* or *Mrs.*)

Always use a married woman's first name, not her husband's. Only in formal social correspondence is using the husband's first and last name (as in *Mrs. John Smith*) still customary—though this approach is fast becoming outdated. And use her correct last name. Be careful—It may be hyphenated (*Joan Summers-Smith*) or completely different from her husband's last name (*Joan Summers*).

Widowed? Divorced? Unless you know that a woman has changed her name on becoming divorced or widowed, continue to use her married name and follow the same preceding guidelines in determining which title (if any) to use.

When addressing several women, avoid the formal *Mlles.* and *Mmes.* (plural forms of *Miss* and *Mrs.*) except in extremely formal or legal correspondence. Instead, list each woman's name in both the inside address and the salutation. When all recipients are women, *Ladies* is also acceptable although somewhat formal.

Address:	Mrs. Jane Smith		Jane Smith
	Miss Sue Jones	*or*	Sue Jones
	Ms. Ann Thomas		Ann Thomas

Salutation: Dear Mrs. Smith, Miss Jones, and Ms. Thomas:

or

Dear Jane Smith, Sue Jones, and Ann Thomas:

or

Dear Jane, Sue, and Ann: (If close relationship)

Couples

Addressing letters to couples these days can be confusing. Married couples with the same last name are the easiest. Here are three options for the inside address, with suggested uses, followed by three options for salutations.

Address: Mr. and Mrs. John Smith
(Still customary in formal social correspondence.)

or

Mr. John and Mrs. Joan Smith
(More modern and unlikely to offend.)

or

John and Joan Smith
(Also modern, widely accepted, and unlikely to offend.)

Salutation: Dear Mr. and Mrs. Smith:

or

Dear John and Joan Smith:

or

Dear John and Joan,

When husband and wife have different last names, when only one name is hyphenated, or in the case of same-sex couples or roommates with different last names, use one of the following two options for the inside address. Three options for the salutation follow.

Address: Mr. John Smith and Ms. Joan Summers-Smith

or

John Smith and Joan Summers-Smith

Salutation: Dear Mr. Smith and Ms. Summers-Smith:

or

Dear John Smith and Joan Summers-Smith:

or

Dear John and Joan,

When one spouse/partner/roommate has a professional title and the other does not, use one of these forms of address:

Husband with title:

Address: Dr. and Mrs. Smith

or

Dr. John and Mrs. Joan Smith

(Dr. John Smith and Mrs. Joan Summers-Smith)

Salutation: Dear Dr. and Mrs. Smith:

(Dear Dr. Smith and Mrs. Summers-Smith:)

Wife with title:

Address: Dr. and Mr. Smith

or

Dr. Joan and Mr. John Smith

(Dr. Joan Summers-Smith and Mr. John Smith)

Salutation: Dear Dr. and Mr. Smith:

(Dear Dr. Summers-Smith and Mr. Smith:)

When both spouse/partner/roommates have titles, use one of these forms of address:

Address: Drs. John and Joan Smith

(Drs. John Smith and Joan Summers-Smith)

or

Drs. Joan and John Smith

(Drs. Joan Summers-Smith and John Smith)

Salutation: Dear Drs. Smith:

(Dear Drs. Smith and Summers-Smith:)

Not sure these days who to list first? Listing a husband's name first is still conventional. Some people prefer instead to list names alphabetically to avoid the issue of who to list first.

Gender or name unknown

If you're writing to an individual whose gender you don't know, don't assume "he's" masculine. The most accepted method of addressing that person is to omit the social title and simply use the person's first and last name (or initials, if initials are all you have).

Address: Terry Smith

or

T.S. Smith

Salutation: Dear Terry Smith:

or

Dear T.S. Smith:

When addressing a generic individual representing a company, organization, or agency, the best (and most gender-sensitive) method to address that person is with a position title:

Address: Customer Service Representative
ABC Corporation

Salutation: Dear Customer Service Representative:

Address: Social Security Representative
Social Security Administration

Salutation: Dear Social Security Representative:

This form of address avoids the masculine *Dear Sir* or *Dear Sirs* approach. *Dear Ladies and Gentlemen* sounds melodramatic in most situations, and *Dear Lady or Gentleman* sounds—well—silly, and even *Dear Sir or Madam* can offend some. (*Sir* commands respect, but *Madam*, for some, conjures up images of sequins and pink feather boas.) And *To Whom It May Concern* sounds as if you're beginning a eulogy!

When deciding on a position title to use, pick as specific a position title as you're sure about. If you're not sure of the position of the person who will receive the letter, choose a more generic title, such as "Agency Representative."

To further ensure that the right person will get your letter, include an attention line as well—both on the envelope and on the letter itself. (See page 43 in Chapter 5.)

Professional titles

Attorney

Address: Mr. John Smith, Attorney-at-Law

or

John Smith, Esq.

Salutation: Dear Mr. Smith:

or

Dear John Smith, Esq.:

When one of the parties of a couple is a lawyer and the other not, place the lawyer's name first to avoid confusion:

Mr. John Smith, Esq., and Mrs. Joan Smith

Mrs. Joan Smith, Attorney-at-Law, and Mr. John Smith

Dentist

Address: Joan Smith, D.D.S.

or

Dr. Joan Smith

Salutation: Dear Dr. Smith:

Physician

Address: John Smith, M.D.

or

Dr. John Smith

Salutation: Dear Dr. Smith:

Veterinarian

Address: Joan Smith, D.V.M.

or

Dr. Joan Smith

Salutation: Dear Dr. Smith:

Corporate titles

While not all business organizations follow an identical hierarchy of positions, a typical company hierarchy is as follows:

Chairperson of the Board

President and/or Chief Executive Officer (CEO)

Chief Operating Officer (COO)

Executive Vice President

Associate Vice President

Vice President

Officer: Comptroller, Corporate Secretary, Treasurer

Director

Manager

Supervisor

When writing to someone in any position on the hierarchy (or to any other representative of the organization, for that matter), your inside address and envelope should include both the person's name, if you know it, and the position title. Specifying the particular department or area of the company is also a good idea. The salutation should include only the name (or only the position title if you do not have a name).

Address: John Smith, Associate Vice President of Finance
ABC Company

Salutation: Dear Mr. Smith:

or

Address: Associate Vice President of Finance
ABC Company

Salutation: Dear Associate Vice President:

Take the time to find out a recipient's name whenever possible. Often a quick phone call to the organization's switchboard receptionist can give you the information you need to add a personal touch that will flatter, and possibly impress, that person—and get your letter more personalized attention.

State and local government titles

Government, at all levels, tends to cherish its formal titles. Use the proper title to get the best results from state and local government officials. Your local library can help you with specific names and addresses.

Alderman/woman or Committeeman/woman

Address: The Honorable Joan Smith or Alderwoman Joan Smith
City Hall

Salutation: Dear Ms. Smith:

Assemblyman/woman

See Representative, State

Commissioner

Address: The Honorable John Smith

Salutation: Dear Mr. Smith:

Governor

Address: The Honorable Joan Smith
Governor of Indiana

Salutation: Dear Ms. Smith:

Lieutenant Governor

Address: The Honorable John Smith
Lieutenant Governor of Indiana

Salutation: Dear Mr. Smith:

Mayor

Address: The Honorable Joan Smith
Mayor of Indianapolis

Salutation: Dear Mayor Smith:

Representative, State

Address: The Honorable John Smith
House of Representatives

Salutation: Dear Mr. Smith:

or

Dear Representative Smith:

Senator, State

Address: The Honorable Jane Smith
The State Senate

Salutation: Dear Ms. Smith:

or

Dear Senator Smith:

U.S. government titles

If an officer of the government has a professional title, such as *Dr.*, substitute it for the social titles *Mr., Mrs., Ms., or Miss.*

Cabinet officers: Secretary of State

Address: The Honorable John Smith
Secretary of State

Salutation: Dear Mr. Smith

or

Dear Secretary Smith:

Cabinet officers: Attorney General

Address: The Honorable Joan Smith
Attorney General of the United States

Salutation: Dear Madam Attorney General:

Committee/Subcommittee Chairs of Senate or House

Address: The Honorable John Smith
Chair
House Ways and Means Committee
United States House of Representatives

Salutation: Dear Mr. Chairman:

or

Dear Representative Smith:

Former U.S. President

Address: The Honorable John Smith

Salutation: Dear Mr. Smith:

President, U.S.

Address: The President
The White House

or

President John Smith
The White House

or

President Smith
The White House

Salutation: Dear Mr. President:

Representative, U.S.

Address: The Honorable Joan Smith
United States House of Representatives

Salutation: Dear Ms. Smith:

or

Dear Representative Smith:

Senator, U.S.

Address: The Honorable John Smith
United States Senate

Salutation: Dear Senator Smith:

Speaker, U.S. House of Representatives

Address: The Honorable Joan Smith
Speaker of the House of Representatives

Salutation: Dear Madam Speaker:

or

Dear Ms. Speaker:

Vice President, U.S.
Address: The Vice President of the United States
or
Vice President Smith
Salutation: Dear Mr. Vice President:
or
Dear Mr. Smith:

U.S., state, and local court titles

Associate Justice, Supreme Court
Address: Madam Justice Smith or Justice Smith
The Supreme Court of the United States
Salutation: Dear Madam Justice:
or
Dear Justice Smith:

Chief Justice, Supreme Court
Address: The Chief Justice of the United States
The Supreme Court of the United States
Salutation: Dear Mr. Chief Justice:
or
Dear Chief Justice Smith:

Judge, federal
Address: The Honorable Joan Smith
United States District Judge
Salutation: Dear Judge Smith:

Judge, state or local
Address: The Honorable John Smith
Chief Judge of the Court of Appeals
Salutation: Dear Judge Smith:

Clerk of a federal or state court
Address: Joan Smith, Esq. or Ms. Joan Smith
Clerk of the Superior Court of Indiana
Salutation: Dear Ms. Smith:

Diplomatic titles

Ambassador to the United States
Address: His Excellency John Smith
The Ambassador of Peru

Salutation: Dear Mr. Ambassador:

or

Your Excellency:

American Ambassador to other countries
Address: The Honorable Joan Smith
Ambassador of the United States

Salutation: Dear Madam Ambassador:

or

Dear Ambassador Smith:

American Chargè d'Affaires
Address: John Smith, Esq.
American Chargè d'Affaires

Salutation: Dear Mr. Smith:

American Minister to other countries
Address: The Honorable Joan Smith
American Minister to Botswana

Salutation: Dear Madam Smith:

or

Dear Minister Smith:

Minister to the United States
Address: The Honorable John Smith
Minister of Botswana

Salutation: Dear Mr. Minister:

or

Dear Minister Smith:

Secretary General, U.N.
Address: Her Excellency Joan Smith
Secretary General of the United Nations

Salutation: Dear Madam Secretary General:

Military titles

Admiral, Vice Admiral, Rear Admiral

Address: Full rank + Full name + Comma + Abbreviated branch of service
(For example: Admiral Jonathan A. Smith, USN)

Salutation: Dear Admiral Smith:

Airman

Address: Full rank + Full name + Comma + Abbreviated branch of service

Salutation: Dear Airman Smith:

Captain

(Air Force, Army, Coast Guard, Marine Corps, or Navy)

Address: Full rank + Full name + Comma + Abbreviated branch of service

Salutation: Dear Captain Smith:

Colonel, Lieutenant Colonel

(Air Force, Army, or Marine Corps)

Address: Full rank + Full name + Comma + Abbreviated branch of service

Salutation: Dear Colonel Smith:

Commander, Commodore

(Coast Guard or Navy)

Address: Full rank + Full name + Comma + Abbreviated branch of service

Salutation: Dear Commander Smith:

Corporal

Address: Full rank + Full name + Comma + Abbreviated branch of service

Salutation: Dear Corporal Smith:

First Lieutenant, Second Lieutenant

(Air Force, Army, or Marine Corps)

Address: Full rank + Full name + Comma + Abbreviated branch of service

Salutation: Dear Lieutenant Smith:

General, Lieutenant General, Major General, Brigadier General

(Air Force, Army, or Marine Corps)

Address: Full rank + Full name + Comma + Abbreviated branch of service

Salutation: Dear General Smith:

Lieutenant Commander

Address: Full rank + Full name + Comma + Abbreviated branch of service

Salutation: Dear Lieutenant Smith:

Lieutenant, Lieutenant Junior Grade, Ensign

(Coast Guard or Navy)

Address: Full rank + Full name + Comma + Abbreviated branch of service

Salutation: Dear Mr. (or Ms.) Smith:

Major

(Air Force, Army, or Marine Corps)

Address: Full rank + Full name + Comma + Abbreviated branch of service

Salutation: Dear Major Smith:

Master Sergeant

(And other enlisted ranks with compound titles)

Address: Full rank + Full name + Comma + Abbreviated branch of service

Salutation: Dear Sergeant Smith:

Midshipman

Address: Midshipman Joan Smith
United States Naval Academy

Salutation: Dear Midshipman Smith:

Petty Officer and Chief Petty Officer ranks

Address: Full rank + Full name + Comma + Abbreviated branch of service

Salutation: Dear Mr. Smith:

or

Dear Chief Smith:

Private

Address: Full rank + Full name + Comma + Abbreviated branch of service

Salutation: Dear Private Smith:

Seaman

Address: Full rank + Full name + Comma + Abbreviated branch of service

Salutation: Dear Seaman Smith:

Specialist

Address: Full rank + Full name + Comma + Abbreviated branch of service

Salutation: Dear Ms. Smith:

Other ranks

Address: Full rank + Full name + Comma + Abbreviated branch of service

Salutation: Dear Mr. Smith:

Military abbreviations

Army	USA
Air Force	USAF
Coast Guard	USCG
Marine Corps	USMC
Navy	USN

Religious titles

Following are titles for clergy of Roman Catholic, Protestant, and Jewish faiths. For religious leaders of Buddhist, Islamic, and Hindu faiths, see notes at the end of this section.

Roman Catholic

Bishop and Archbishop

Address: The Most Reverend John Smith, D.D.
Bishop (Archbishop) of Indianapolis

Salutation: Dear Bishop (Archbishop):

or

Your Excellency:

Cardinal

Address: His Eminence, John Cardinal Smith
Archbishop of Seattle

Salutation: Dear Cardinal Smith:

or

Your Eminence:

Monsignor

Address: Reverend Msgr. John Smith

Salutation: Dear Monsignor Smith:

or

Reverend Monsignor:

Nun

Some sisters prefer to be addressed by their last, rather than their first, name. Use her preferred form, if you know it.

Address: Sister Joan Smith

Salutation: Dear Sister:

or

Dear Sister Joan:

The Pope
    Address: His Holiness, The Pope
                  or
              His Holiness, Pope John Smith
              Vatican City
    Salutation: Your Holiness:
                  or
              Most Holy Father:

Priest
    Address: The Reverend John Smith
    Salutation: Dear Father Smith:

Protestant
Archbishop
    Address: The Most Reverend Archbishop of New York
                  or
              The Most Reverend John Smith
              Archbishop of New York
    Salutation: Dear Archbishop Smith:
                  or
              Your Grace:

Archdeacon
    Address: The Venerable John Smith
              Archdeacon of Los Angeles
    Salutation: Dear Archdeacon:
                  or
              Venerable Sir:

Bishop
    Address: The Right Reverend Joan Smith
              Bishop of Paterson
               or
              The Reverend Joan Smith
    Salutation: Dear Bishop Smith:
                  or
              Right Reverend Madam:
                  or
              Reverend Madam:

Dean (Head of Cathedral or Theological Seminary)

Address: The Very Reverend Warren C. Farrell
Dean of Christian Theological Seminary

Salutation: Dear Dean Farrell:

or

Very Reverend Sir:

Priest or Minister

Address: The Reverend Joan Smith

Salutation: Dear Reverend Smith:

Jewish

Rabbi

Address: Rabbi John Smith

or

Rabbi John Smith, Ph.D.

Salutation: Dear Rabbi Smith:

or

Dear Dr. Smith:

Buddhist, Islamic, Hindu

Because these religions have no formal clerical hierarchy, contact a temple or mosque for more specific information before addressing an individual in these faiths.

Buddhist

Most forms of Buddhism, except Tibetan Buddhism, have no formal religious hierarchy. Tibetan Buddhists follow a Dalai Lama, addressed as *His Holiness.*

Buddhist monks, nuns, and priests may be addressed with their full name, followed by an honorary title, if they have one, such as *rinpoche: Wan Chen Rinpoche.*

Islamic

The head of a mosque is referred to as an *Imam*; other religious scholars and teachers are given the honorary title *mullah.* Use the honorary title and full name of the person you wish to address: *Imam Mohamad Ulhaq Azziz.*

Hindu

Those individuals recognized as spiritually developed receive honorary titles. Few people have received the title *Mahatma (Great Soul).* Guru *(Spiritual Guide)* applies to one who instructs students in spiritual disciplines. Use the full name of the person you wish to address, preceded by the honorary title: *Guru Rama Chopra.*

College and university titles

In each case, the individual's academic degrees, if you know them, may be added after the name.

Dean

Address: Dean Joan Smith, Ph.D.
Salutation: Dear Dean Smith, Ph.D.:

President

Address: President John Smith
Salutation: Dear President Smith:

Professor

Address: Professor Joan Smith
Salutation: Dear Professor Smith:

CHAPTER 7

Letter and Envelope Formats

To ensure that your letter is well-received, and out of convenience to the recipient of your letter, you'll want to follow an accepted format, or way to lay it out on the page. Modern computer word-processing programs, with their letter and envelope templates and their automatic page formats, can greatly help you with this, but they do not cover every possible form of letter or envelope that you might need. (And please note, much of what is discussed in this chapter does not apply to e-mail, which does not require an envelope, as we all know!)

Your job here would be substantially simpler if there were only one possible format. In fact, you have several options. We've attempted to simplify the options, but essentially you have six format options from which to choose: two if your letter is strictly social in nature and four if you want to conduct business with a letter.

In addition to laying out the six formats, this chapter will cover other issues of format, namely:

- Should I hand-write or type my letter? (Does it matter?)

- What size and color paper should I use: standard 8 1/2 x 11 white paper or my smaller, colored stationery?

- Is preprinted letterhead better than typing or writing out my address?

- How do I format a second page?

- How do I address the envelope?

Forms of address, or how to correctly address individuals of different genders and in various professions and environments, is complicated enough to warrant a separate chapter. For forms of address, see Chapter 6.

Business letter formats

To accomplish most personal business with an organization, a volunteer or civic group, or sometimes even one individual, use a business letter format. A business letter format is usually more appropriate than a social format when your goal is *getting something done*. Your personal business could include anything from complaining about your telephone service to notifying your bank of an error to resigning from a volunteer position to disputing your plumber's bill.

Business letters typically follow one of four basic formats:

1. Block.

2. Modified block.

3. Modified semiblock.

4. Simplified.

With the exception of the simplified format, business letter formats vary primarily in where you place the date and the complimentary close. Which format you choose is strictly a matter of personal preference. Many people prefer the simplicity of the block format, in which all text lines up flush with the left margin, while others prefer the more balanced look of modified block or modified semiblock, in which the date and complimentary close are positioned just right of center.

The simplified letter format, which omits both the salutation and the complimentary close, might sound like a tempting format shortcut, but you'll probably opt against using it, as letters written in this format come across as abrupt and impersonal. This format is generally reserved for sales form letters sent by big organizations.

For purposes of demonstration, we have chosen to vary the format of the sample business letters in the latter part of this book using the block, modified block, and modified semiblock formats.

Block format

The block format is the best combination of a simple approach and a professional look. All text begins at the left margin, and spaces separate both the paragraphs and the various letter parts.

James Thompson
765 Brookfield Lane
Anytown, Illinois 12345-5431

January 21, 2004

Reference: Account Number 788-4509

Sandra Jamison, Customer Service Representative
Ames Department Store
85 Keystone Avenue
Anytown, Illinois 12345-5431

Attention: Customer Service Manager

Dear Ms. Jamison:

Subject: XXXXXXXXXX

XXXXXXXXXXXXXXXXXXXXXXXXXXXXXXXXXXXXXXXXXX
XXXXXXXXXXXXXXXXXXXXXXXXXXXXXXXXXXXXXXXX
XXXXXXXXXXXXXXXXXXXXXXXXXXXXXXXXXXXXXXXXX
XXXXXXXXXXXXXXXXXX

XXXXXXXXXXXXXXXXXXXXXXXXXXXXXXXXXXXXXXXXX
XXXXXXXXXXXXXXXXXXXXXXXXXXXXXXXXXXXXXXXXXXX
XXXXXXXXXXXXXXXXXXXXXXXXXXXXXXXXX

Sincerely,

James Thompson

Receipt enclosed

Modified block format

In a modified block format, as in block format, most parts of the letter begin at the left margin, and spaces separate both the paragraphs and the various letter parts. But with modified block, the date, complimentary close, and signature begin near the center of the letter, creating a more balanced look.

James Thompson
765 Brookfield Lane
Anytown, Illinois 12345-5431

January 21, 2004

Reference: Account Number 788-4509

Sandra Jamison, Customer Service Representative
Ames Department Store
85 Keystone Avenue
Anytown, Illinois 12345-5431

Attention: Customer Service Manager

Dear Ms. Jamison:

Subject: XXXXXXXXXX

XXXXXXXXXXXXXXXXXXXXXXXXXXXXXXXXXXXXXXXXX
XXXXXXXXXXXXXXXXXXXXXXXXXXXXXXXXXXXXXXX
XXXXXXXXXXXXXXXXXXXXXXXXXXXXXXXXXXXXXXXX
XXXXXXXXXXXXXXXXX

XXXXXXXXXXXXXXXXXXXXXXXXXXXXXXXXXXXXXXXXX
XXXXXXXXXXXXXXXXXXXXXXXXXXXXXXXXXXXXXXXXXX
XXXXXXXXXXXXXXXXXXXXXXXXXXXXXXXXXXXX

Sincerely,

James Thompson

Receipt enclosed

Modified semiblock format

Modified semiblock format is identical to modified block except that each new paragraph is indented five spaces. All other spacing in the letter remains the same as modified block.

James Thompson
765 Brookfield Lane
Anytown, Illinois 12345-5431

January 21, 2004

Reference: Account Number 788-4509

Sandra Jamison, Customer Service Representative
Ames Department Store
85 Keystone Avenue
Anytown, Illinois 12345-5431

Attention: Customer Service Manager

Dear Ms. Jamison:

Subject: XXXXXXXXX

    XXXXXXXXXXXXXXXXXXXXXXXXXXXXXXXXXXXX
XXXXXXXXXXXXXXXXXXXXXXXXXXXXXXXXXXXX
XXXXXXXXXXXXXXXXXXXXXXXXXXXXXXXXXXXXX
XXXXXXXXXXXXXXXXX

    XXXXXXXXXXXXXXXXXXXXXXXXXXXXXXXXXXX
XXXXXXXXXXXXXXXXXXXXXXXXXXXXXXXXXXXXXXXXX
XXXXXXXXXXXXXXXXXXXXXXXXXXXXXXXX

Sincerely,

James Thompson

Receipt enclosed

Simplified format

The simplified letter format is similar to block format. All text begins at the left margin, and spaces separate both the paragraphs and the various letter parts. But the simplified format omits both the salutation and the complimentary close.

This format certainly eliminates the need to know your recipient's gender (for the correct courtesy title) or even your recipient's name. However, it tends to give your letter an abrupt, impersonal feel. For alternative ways of handling problems with people's names, see Chapter 6.

James Thompson
765 Brookfield Lane
Anytown, Illinois 12345-5431

January 21, 2004

Reference: Account Number 788-4509

Sandra Jamison, Customer Service Representative
Ames Department Store
85 Keystone Avenue
Anytown, Illinois 12345-5431

Attention: Customer Service Manager

Subject: XXXXXXXXXX

XXXXXXXXXXXXXXXXXXXXXXXXXXXXXXXXXXXXXXXXX
XXXXXXXXXXXXXXXXXXXXXXXXXXXXXXXXXXXXXXX
XXXXXXXXXXXXXXXXXXXXXXXXXXXXXXXXXXXXXXXX
XXXXXXXXXXXXXXXX

XXXXXXXXXXXXXXXXXXXXXXXXXXXXXXXXXXXXXXXX
XXXXXXXXXXXXXXXXXXXXXXXXXXXXXXXXXXXXXXXXXXX
XXXXXXXXXXXXXXXXXXXXXXXXXXXXXXXXXXX

James Thompson

Receipt enclosed

Social letter formats

Social letter formats should (perhaps obviously) be used for social, less formal purposes, from congratulating a close friend to consoling a grieving business associate to thanking a top-notch teacher. You'll probably use a social format most often with people you know.

Formats used for social letters are simpler than those used for business letters. Because they're more typically written to one individual and received by a household versus an organization, social letters usually omit the formalities of an inside address, the typed signature line, and most of the special notations included in business letters (reference line, mail or confidential notations, attention line, subject line, and additional notations).

The two types of social letter formats vary only in terms of their simplicity:

1. Standard social format.

2. Intimate format.

As the name of the second social format implies, it is appropriate only for the most familiar recipients and the most intimate situations. For demonstration purposes, we have varied the format of the sample letters in the latter part of this book between the two styles above.

Standard social format

In the standard social format, the sender's address (typically without the sender's name), date, complimentary close, and signature begin near the center of the letter. Each new paragraph is typically indented.

Because social letters are more often hand-written than typed, the space between paragraphs may be omitted; however, your letter will be easier to read with the spaces left in.

---

765 Brookfield Lane
Anytown, Illinois 12345-5431
March 10, 2004

Dear Sam,

XXXXXXXXXXXXXXXXXXXXXXXXXXXXXXXXXXXXXXXXX
XXXXXXXXXXXXXXXXXXXXXXXXXXXXXXXXXXXXXXXXXXX
XXXXXXXXXXXXXXXXXXXXXXXXXXXXXXXXXXXXXXX
XXXXXXXXXXXXXXX

XXXXXXXXXXXXXXXXXXXXXXXXXXXXXXXXXXXXXX
XXXXXXXXXXXXXXXXXXXXXXXXXXXXXXXXXXXXXXXX
XXXXXXXXXXXXXXXXXXXXXXXXXXXXXX

XXXXXXXXXXXXXXXXXXXXXXXXXXXXXXXXXXXX
XXXXXXXXXXXXXXXXXXXXXXXXXXXXXXXXXXXXXXXX
XXXXXXXXXXXXXXXXXXXXXXXXXXXXXXXXXXXXXXX
XXXXXXXXXXXXXXXXXXXXXXXXXXXXXXXXXX

Very truly yours,

Jim

Intimate format

For an intimate touch in a letter to someone with whom you have a very close relationship, use the intimate format—an abbreviated version of the standard social format. The intimate format omits the sender's address and begins with the date in the upper corner, just to the right of center.

March 10, 2004

Dear Sam,

XXXXXXXXXXXXXXXXXXXXXXXXXXXXXXXXXXXXXX
XXXXXXXXXXXXXXXXXXXXXXXXXXXXXXXXXXXXXXXXX
XXXXXXXXXXXXXXXXXXXXXXXXXXXXXXXXXXXXXXX
XXXXXXXXXXXXXXX

XXXXXXXXXXXXXXXXXXXXXXXXXXXXXXXXXXXXX
XXXXXXXXXXXXXXXXXXXXXXXXXXXXXXXXXXXXX
XXXXXXXXXXXXXXXXXXXXXXXXXXXXXX

XXXXXXXXXXXXXXXXXXXXXXXXXXXXXXXXXXXXX
XXXXXXXXXXXXXXXXXXXXXXXXXXXXXXXXXXXXXXXXX
XXXXXXXXXXXXXXXXXXXXXXXXXXXXXXXXXXXXXXXXX
XXXXXXXXXXXXXXXXXXXXXXXXXXXXXXXXXXX

Very truly yours,

Jim

Format questions and answers

Following are the most commonly asked questions people have about the appropriate format of their social and business-oriented personal letters. The answers are designed to enhance *your* letter's effectiveness.

Q: Should my letter be typed or written out by hand?

A: Either is appropriate, depending on what you want to accomplish. Business-oriented letters tend to carry more weight typed—especially if the topic is a serious one or you've written to this individual or organization on this issue before. A less formal business letter (for instance, a letter accompanying a straightforward merchandise return or a letter to your child's third-grade teacher) might be quite appropriately written out by hand. Social letters, especially intimate social letters, are nearly always handwritten and might appear less than sincere if you type them.

Q: What size and color paper should I use, and does that really matter?

A: Again, the answer depends on whether your purpose is to conduct personal business or to drop a social note. Business-oriented correspondence, especially those letters dealing with serious or persistent issues or those going to a formal or professional business environment (and *always* letters accompanying resumes or curriculum vitaes), are most appropriately written on standard 8 1/2 x 11 paper.

White paper is standard, of course, and tends to best convey business formality. Off-white, buff, or pale grey paper is also acceptable for very formal business situations such as a cover letter and resume/vitae, a formal invitation, or a formal thank you. Generally speaking, stick to white for most personal business purposes.

Social letters offer more flexibility in terms of both size and color of paper. For most social purposes, your best bet is a tasteful stationery with little or no design in just about any pale color and a size big enough to hold what you have to say.

Q: Is preprinted letterhead better than typing or writing out my address?

A: Letterhead is certainly more impressive than an address typed or written out if, again, the business-oriented topic is a serious one or if you've written to this individual or organization on this issue before. For most business purposes, a typed address will suffice though typing it out is certainly more work. My advice: If you don't have stationery with letterhead, create a simple template on your computer (many word-processing programs have a special tool to guide you). It will look just as good!

Hand-written addresses work best with hand-written social letters or hand-written business letters going to a less formal business environment. (Catalog return departments, for instance, generally receive hand-written letters.)

Even your most intimate social letters typically do not include the sender's address. So the advantage of social stationery with letterhead is that your letter will appear just as intimate, and the recipient will have no question whom the letter is from!

Q: How do I format a second page?

A: If your business-oriented letter goes to a second page, first make sure you can't condense it to one page. Two-page business letters look less enticing to read, and many people set them aside on infamous "I'll get around to it later" piles.

If you cannot avoid a second page, follow these business format guidelines:

- Use the same style of paper as you used on page one but without the letterhead.

- Keep the margins on page two the same as those on page one.

- Avoid indicating "continued," "cont'd.," or "over" on page one. Instead, list the recipient's name as it appeared in the inside address, the date fully spelled out, and the page number at the top of page two, using one of the following two format options (the second of which is more commonly used):

  Across the top of the page:
  Sandra Jamison   January 21, 2004   page 2

  At the left margin:
  Sandra Jamison
  January 21, 2004
  page two

- Avoid leaving a single line of text on either page. Move a two- or three-line paragraph to one page or the other.

- Avoid starting the second page with just the complimentary close; move the last two or three lines of the letter's body to page two and then add the close.

- Avoid dividing the last word of the letter's text between pages one and two. Move the last two or three lines of page one to page two as suggested above.

  These same guidelines are also appropriate for social letters. The only exception is the format for starting page two: In social letters, a centered page number at the top of the page is all that's needed.

Q: What about margins? Do the size of the margins matter?

A: Margins matter for a couple of reasons. First, symmetrical, consistent margins give any letter a pleasing look and suggest a conscientious letter-writer.

Second, especially in business-oriented letters, margins can help text to appear more balanced on a page; short letters should use wider margins (at most 2"), and longer letters should use more narrow margins (typically no less than 1"). Use top and bottom margins, too, to help the text appear centered or slightly high on the page.

Q: How do I correctly address the envelope?

A: Envelope-addressing formats have changed in recent years largely because of the U.S. Postal Service's use of automated optical character readers (OCRs). If you want your letter to arrive quickly and without problems, you would be well served to follow the post office guidelines to the extent you feel comfortable doing so.

The post office's suggested format breaks from convention and certainly isn't the most personal or aesthetically-pleasing approach, but it will get the letter to its destination. Each of us is left to decide which is more important— conveying a warm, personal first impression or getting the letter to its recipient most effectively and efficiently.

OCRs handle typed text best, of course; but they can also read carefully formed printed and even some script letters, depending on how conventionally you write. Here are the post office's guidelines for surest handling of your letters:

- Send envelopes no smaller than 3 1/2 x 5 inches.

- Use typed or printed text, in all capitals, without any punctuation.

- Make "attention" lines the first line of the address (when you use them), rather than the last line. Write out the word "attention" or abbreviate it "attn"; either way, omit all punctuation.

- Use standard two-letter state abbreviations and zip codes—including the additional four digits when you have them.

- List the address to which you want the letter delivered *last* (when you have more than one address, a street address and a post office box, for instance). OCRs read information from right to left, down to up; your letter will go to the address you list last, which it reads first.

Here is how the post office would like your envelope to appear:

SUZANNE JONES
10075 42ND AVE
ROCHESTER CT zip+4

ATTENTION JAMES MERRIMAN
BILLING DEPARTMENT
CROSSFIELD PRODUCTS
10 CHAMPION LANE
PLAINFIELD MA zip+4

Standard two-letter state abbreviations

Alabama	AL	Montana	MT
Alaska	AK	Nebraska	NE
Arizona	AZ	Nevada	NV
Arkansas	AR	New Hampshire	NH
California	CA	New Jersey	NJ
Colorado	CO	New Mexico	NM
Connecticut	CT	New York	NY
Delaware	DE	North Carolina	NC
District of Columbia	DC	North Dakota	ND
Florida	FL	Ohio	OH
Georgia	GA	Oklahoma	OK
Hawaii	HI	Oregon	OR
Idaho	ID	Pennsylvania	PA
Illinois	IL	Puerto Rico	PR
Indiana	IN	Rhode Island	RI
Iowa	IO	South Carolina	SC
Kansas	KS	South Dakota	SD
Kentucky	KY	Tennessee	TN
Louisiana	LA	Texas	TX
Maine	ME	Utah	UT
Maryland	MD	Vermont	VT
Massachusetts	MA	Virginia	VA
Michigan	MI	Washington	WA
Minnesota	MN	West Virginia	WV
Mississippi	MS	Wisconsin	WI
Missouri	MO	Wyoming	WY

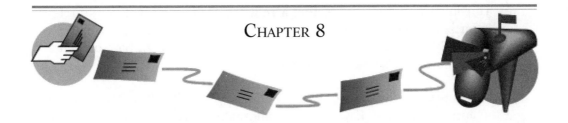

CHAPTER 8

Templates for Successful Letters and E-mails

In Chapter 4, we proposed that most letters or e-mails you write seek to accomplish one of only six basic purposes. Simply identify the type of letter you're writing by its primary, overriding purpose, and you'll be better able to choose the letter template, or recommended strategy, that will best get the job done.

The most effective letters attempt to accomplish one, ideally, and no more than two purposes in any one letter. Here, again, are those six basic purposes.

1. **To request information or routine action from someone.** From "Please repair my watch under warranty" to "Send me an application," to "Please provide guidelines for recycling in my neighborhood," these letters are typically less emotionally-charged and fairly straightforward to write.

2. **To persuade someone to take action.** This action can be anything from "Consider me for a position" to "Resolve my complaint." These letters address more than routine requests and those in which you might suspect some resistance from the reader.

3. **To demand action.** These letters are appropriate after a kinder request or two, by phone or otherwise, didn't do the job.

4. **To provide information or describe action you have taken or an event affecting you.** Often these letters respond to a request someone has made of you ("Here is transcript you requested"), but they may also describe your independent action ("I resign as committee chair"). If your true purpose is merely to provide information, you expect no further action.

5. **To acknowledge action someone else has taken or an event affecting that person.** Holiday greetings fall into this category, as do recognition, congratulation, and thank-you letters. A letter acknowledging receipt of some message or product also achieves this purpose.

6. **To convey bad news or decline a request.** Delivering bad news in a letter is no picnic. It must be done with tact and kindness. Saying no gracefully when someone has make a request you must, or have chosen to, decline can also be challenging.

In this chapter, we'll cover the six templates in detail. These templates are suggested approaches only. If you've used alternate approaches and had success with them, use them! You can use these templates for crafting an e-mail message, too, not just for a traditional letter. Although we refer only to letters throughout this chapter, freely apply what pertains to your particular e-mail message.

Template 1: To request information or routine action

These letters are perhaps the most straightforward to write. They are typically the first letter you will write to address the issue at hand, and because they deal with a routine request, they generally do not require heavy persuasion. These letters should respect the recipient's time by quickly naming the information or action you desire.

Step 1:	Request the information or action you want early in the first paragraph.
Step 2:	Cover any background information or details relevant to your request. Make sure everything you discuss will seem relevant and important to your reader as well. If this information is extensive, consider ways of making it easy to find, such as a bulleted list of points, for instance, or a numbered sequence of events.
Step 3:	State or restate any specific information the recipient might need to comply with your request, including an address to respond to, a response deadline, a phone number in the case of questions, and so on.
Step 4:	Reiterate your request and/or thank the recipient.

Template 1 sample

Julie Robinson
1 S. Broadway Avenue
Anytown, Missouri 12345-1234

January 18, 2004

County Extension Representative
Jefferson County Extension Office
77 Jefferson Square
Anytown, Missouri 12345-1234

Dear Extension Representative:

Your Master Gardener program, featured in this past Sunday's *Star* newspaper, really interests me. Could you please send me information about how I can get involved?

The article explained the cost for classes; I now need more information on where and when classes are being held, whether I can jump into a series already in progress, and what happens if I must miss a class or two. (Must I pass a test at the end of a series?)

Please send me any information you feel I would find valuable, or if faxing information is easier for you, please do so: 555-1800. You can also send an e-mail to jrobinson@email.ttt.

Thank you for your time, and I look forward to receiving more information on the Master Gardener program!

Sincerely yours,

Julie Robinson

Template 2: To persuade someone to take action

When the action you want from someone isn't a routine request or you suspect that he or she might resist taking the action you seek, a persuasive letter is called for.

Should you get right to the point in a persuasive letter?

Many people have the impression that when you're trying to persuade someone of something, the best approach is to build up to your request gradually, much as when someone trying to sell you a cell phone unlimited calling package won't tell you the price until he or she has fully explained all the reasons the package would be just right for you.

This build-up approach works in a letter only when your request—your "sales pitch"—is not one your reader is expecting. Your request may, at first glance, seem very unusual, outside the norm of what he or she would expect to find in this letter. A letter to a restaurant owner asking her to give away free food might only succeed if the letter delays the request until it first explains all the benefits for doing so (service to the poor, excellent community image, and so on). Because the restaurant owner will probably view this request as atypical given her usual business dealings with vendors and the like, this letter may need to slowly warm her up to the idea.

But let's say you're writing to the owner of a watch repair service. You want him to repair your 10-year-old watch, no longer under warranty, and you feel he should repair it for free. Now your request may or may not be a fair one, but, chances are, this repair service gets requests at least similar to yours all the time. In this case, *start with the request.* Waiting to state your actual request and expecting him to start by reading paragraph after paragraph of your reasoning will probably frustrate him. *Remember, he deals with this type of request all the time!* Get to the point first before getting into the details.

Most persuasive letters won't come as a surprise to their recipients. Even if the request is unreasonable, these letters work best when they start with the request.

Step 1: State your request in tactful but direct language: "Please repair the enclosed watch without any further charge." Make your request early in your first paragraph. Avoid the temptation to get into lengthy explanations or rationale here.

Step 2: State your reasoning here, probably your second paragraph, after you've stated your request. Cover any details or background information—but make sure these will seem relevant and important to your reader! If this information is extensive, consider ways of making it easy to find: a bulleted list of points, for instance, or a numbered sequence of events.

Step 3: State or restate any specific details the recipient would need to comply with your request, such as an address to respond to, a response deadline, a contact number in the case of questions, and so forth.

Tip: To make a response more likely, provide contact options likely to help your recipient respond easily. A phone number or e-mail address might make responding easier, and you're more likely to get a response more quickly.

Step 4: Thank the recipient, and reiterate your request demonstrating confidence it will be answered: "Thank you for your understanding in this matter. Unless I hear from you to the contrary, I look forward to receiving my repaired watch from you within the next few weeks."

Tip: Start with a subordinate clause ("unless I hear from you to the contrary") to acknowledge but downplay a possible adverse response.

Template 2 sample

Jim Hammer
8011 North Washington Lane
Anytown, Indiana 76543-2314

May 3, 2004

Mr. Timothy Mills, President
Rite Time Watch Repair
10299 North Clinton Road
Anytown, Indiana 76543-2314

Dear Mr. Mills:

Subject: Repaired watch still losing time

Please repair the enclosed watch without any further charge.

You repaired this watch two months ago, and it kept accurate time for several weeks. Since then, however, I seem to be losing 15-20 minutes every day. If I reset the watch each morning, I can get by with it fairly well, but I really need this problem corrected.

Because this seems to be the same problem for which I originally brought it to you, and because I've paid you for the repair, I would expect you to fix this problem without any further charge.

I've enclosed a copy of my receipt for the original repair. If you are unable to comply with my request or have further questions about my watch, please call me at 555-1888 or send an e-mail to jhammer@email.ttt.

Thank you for your understanding in this matter. Unless I hear from you to the contrary, I look forward to receiving my repaired watch from you within the next few weeks.

Sincerely,

Jim Hammer

Watch and repair receipt enclosed

Template 3: To demand action

If your previous requests for action, made by phone or letter, didn't result in action, a stronger letter may be warranted. Letters demanding action are most appropriate after two initial attempts have failed and a reasonable amount of time has passed. We try to give anyone the benefit of the doubt after a phone call, e-mail, or first letter; then we'll "remind" someone of our request with a first or second letter (structured following Template 1 or Template 2).

Only after these attempts have failed do we send a letter using Template 3.

Step 1:	State your letter's purpose and tactfully acknowledge that you have not received a response to your previous request(s): "I am concerned that I have not received a response to my two previous letters (dated XX/XX/XX and XX/XX/XX). I would greatly appreciate your prompt attention to this situation."
	Tip: Avoid beginning your letter with empty phrases such as "I am writing this letter to...," "This letter serves as...," or "The purpose of this letter is to...."
	Tip: To handle situations tactfully, state objective facts from your perspective, state in terms of "I" versus "you" messages, and state potentially blameful statements in the passive voice.
Step 2:	Restate your concern or request.
Step 3:	State your expectations directly and clearly. If warranted, state the next step you are prepared to take if these expectations are not met: "If I do not hear from you by XX/XX/XX, I will take my concerns to your local Better Business Bureau and local chamber of commerce."
Step 4:	Repeat any specific information the recipient might need to comply with your request, such as an address to respond to, a phone number in the case of questions, and so on.
Step 5:	Reiterate your request. Optional: Thank the recipient for his or her cooperation. "I look forward to receiving my repaired watch from you by XX/XX/XX."

Template 3 sample

Jim Hammer
8011 North Washington Lane
Anytown, Indiana 76543-2314

June 30, 2004

Mr. Timothy Mills, President
Rite Time Watch Repair
10299 North Clinton Road
Anytown, Indiana 76543-2314

Dear Mr. Mills:

I am concerned that I have not received a response to either my letter (dated May 3, 2004) or telephone calls (June 6, 15, and 18) about a watch I sent back to you for further repair. I would greatly appreciate your prompt attention to this situation.

My watch was losing time just two months after its repair in your shop in early March. On May 3, I sent the watch back to you to have the problem resolved. I expected the repair to be done within just a few weeks; nearly two months have passed, and I now must insist on receiving my watch back from you as soon as possible.

In fact, if I don't receive either my watch or a telephone call from you explaining the delay by July 10, I will be forced to take my concerns to the management of Northbrook Mall and the local Better Business Bureau.

Again, you can reach me by telephone at 555-1888.

Thank you, and I look forward to receiving either your call or my repaired watch no later than July 10.

Sincerely,

Jim Hammer
555-1888

Template 4: To provide information or describe an event

When instead of requesting information or action, you are in the position of providing it, here's a basic template for doing so quickly and effectively. This template works any time the information you're conveying is good, or at least neutral, news. Bad news typically needs softening and is better addressed with Template 6.

Step 1: State the purpose of your letter, typically a brief overview of the information or event you'll be describing, early in the first paragraph.

Your first paragraph should also make clear whether or not you're writing this letter in response to someone's request for action or information: "In our conversation last week, you asked me to send you information about Bobby's performance at his last school. Here is that information."

Step 2: Provide the information or describe the event. Organize lengthy information in a manner your letter's recipient will find most useful. This may not be a chronological listing of events.

Step 3: Invite the recipient to contact you for more information, if doing so seems appropriate, and provide your address (if not already in your letterhead), telephone number, and/or e-mail address.

Step 4: End your letter with any lasting impression you'd like to leave: "Thank you for taking such an active interest in my son's school performance. I'm sure you'll find he's dedicated to doing his very best at his new school."

Tip: People tend to remember first whatever they read last in a letter. Make your last line count.

Template 4 sample

Sarah Wasserstein
33 Plymouth Boulevard
Anytown, New Jersey 98765-4321

September 8, 2004

Grace Nelson, Acting Principal
New Ridge County Day School
10 Ellen Wood Lane
Anytown, New Jersey 98765-4321

Dear Grace Nelson:

In our conversation last week, you asked me to send you information about Bobby's performance at his last school. Here is that information.

Bobby is an outstanding student academically. Here are his grade point averages for (out of a possible 4.0) grades 3, 4, and 5. A detailed transcript of his grades for these years is attached.

Grade 3	3.72
Grade 4	3.66
Grade 5	3.80

In addition to doing well academically, Bobby sang in his school choir for two years, played soccer for three, and has recently developed an interest in school plays.

If you need further information about my son's performance at his last school, please call me 867-5432 (days) or 867-2345 (evenings). You may also send an e-mail to swasserstein@newridge.ttt.

Thank you for taking such an active interest in my son's school performance. I'm sure you'll find he's dedicated to doing his very best at New Ridge County Day School.

Kind regards,

Sarah Wasserstein

Attached: Westfield County school transcripts (3 pages)

Template 5: To acknowledge information or an event

Use Template 5 to acknowledge service, receipt of information, or a kindness someone has shown you.

Step 1: Immediately and directly acknowledge the information or event: "I received, with regret, your letter of resignation from our neighborhood Crime Watch committee."

Step 2: Elaborate, as appropriate, on any relevant background or details: "Thank you for two years of constant dedication to the cause of increased safety on our block. You've been a dedicated member of the committee, and your actions have greatly contributed to our entire neighborhood's safety." Make sure this information will seem relevant and important to your reader.

Step 3: End your letter with any lasting impression you'd like to leave: "The entire committee will be sad to see you go."

Template 5 sample

Harry Todd
1802 46th Avenue
Anytown, New Jersey 23456

July 13, 2004

Grace Nelson
1884 46th Avenue
Anytown, New Jersey 23456

Dear Grace:

I received, with regret, your letter of resignation from our neighborhood Crime Watch committee.

Thank you for two years of constant dedication to the cause of increased safety on our block. You've been a dedicated member of the committee, and your actions have greatly contributed to our neighborhood's safety.

The entire committee will be sad to see you go.

Yours truly,

Harry Todd

Template 6: To convey bad news or decline a request

Delivering bad news in a letter must be done with tact and kindness. Saying no without offending or discouraging the person you are refusing can also be a difficult task. These are, in fact, some of the few situations in which you might want to delay getting to your letter's point.

Step 1: Start with a general statement about the situation or a restatement of the request.

Step 2: Provide the rationale, as objectively as you can, behind your negative response or bad news. Make sure this information will seem relevant and important to your reader.

Step 3: State the letter's point—the actual bad news or the negative response.

Step 4: If an apology is warranted, make it here in the middle of the letter's body.

Step 5: End your letter on a sincere positive or encouraging note.

Template 6 sample

Grace Nelson
1884 46th Avenue
Anytown, New Jersey 23456

July 6, 2004

Harry Todd
1802 46th Avenue
Anytown, New Jersey 23456

Dear Harry:

As you know, Crime Watch requires a lot of time and energy to make it work for our neighborhood.

And time really comes at a premium for me these days. My two children are in school full-time (which means soccer practices, band practices, you know the routine), and I've recently taken on more responsibilities at New Ridge County Day School, where I previously taught and now serve as acting principal. In my "time off," I'm also busy helping my husband to get his new home-based business off the ground.

In short, I'm afraid I find it necessary to resign from the Crime Watch committee, effective immediately. I simply no longer have the time to be of benefit to the committee.

As I mentioned to you on the phone, I'm sorry I won't be able to help you plan our fall full-block meeting.

I'm sure the committee will continue to make a difference to our neighborhood. I, for one, really appreciate the committee's continued dedication to our cause.

Cordially,

Grace

Look for these six templates accompanying the sample letters in each remaining chapter of this book. The templates help provide a framework for customizing the sample to suit your letter's needs or composing your own letter from scratch.

Sample Letters
and
E-mail Messages

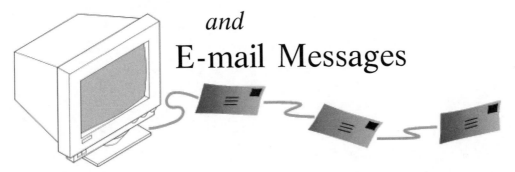

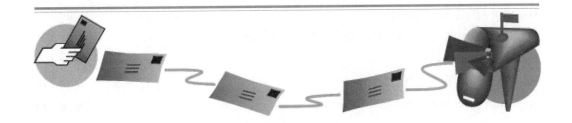

Job and Career Letters
and E-mails

First impressions are critical in letters that seek to land a job or otherwise advance your (or help someone else's) career. Cover letters give a potential employer an immediate image of you and demonstrate how you think, communicate, and conduct business. If your cover letter impresses an employer, he or she is more likely to take a closer look at your resume (or curriculum vitae). A rambling, poorly written, unprofessional letter communicates that you have little regard for what your resume contains.

All of these mandates hold true for e-mailed cover letters and resumes, but be sure to read "Precautions on career-related e-mail," on page 19, for special tips.

Important note: The more you find out about a particular job, the organization offering the job, and your potential employer, the stronger your application letter will likely be. So first take the time to gather information before you write your application or cover letter. For help with your resume, see *Resumes! Resumes! Resumes!* by the editors of Career Press.

Job and career letter samples

For information-gathering and requests: Template 1

If your goal is to make a routine, job-related request of someone, use Template 1. Requesting an interview in which to gather information about a profession, job, or an organization, for instance, calls for Template 1.

But don't use Template 1 to apply for a job. Many people mistakenly think that the purpose of a job-seeking letter is to simply provide information (about one's qualifications, for instance). Instead, think of these as persuasive letters. If they're to be effective, they should indeed be persuasive.

Requesting an informational interview

When someone working in a particular field, position, or organization seems a perfect source for your information-gathering, consider sending a letter requesting an informational interview. Experienced professionals often welcome such interviews as a way to help newcomers to a field or profession.

Kyle Hardeson
6775 Bricklane Place
Olde Towne, Virginia 65432-1256

May 25, 2004

Ms. Ellen Taylor, Instructional Designer
Performance Training Systems
100 Government Avenue
Capital City, D.C. 76543

Dear Ms. Taylor:

Step 1: Request specific information or action.

Eliot Abramson suggested that I write to you. Would you consider meeting with me to discuss the field of instructional design and your experiences in the profession?

Step 2: Cover relevant background and details.

Eliot suggested you might have some great advice for me. I am a computer technologist who became enticed by the field of instructional design about six months ago. I'm now seriously considering an instructional design position at my company, Applied Technologies, and perhaps even returning to school to pursue an advanced degree in the field.

Step 3: Provide contact information

If you wish to call me, my number at Applied Technologies is 111/555-8721. Or please allow me to call you in the next week to see if we might schedule a meeting at your convenience.

Step 4: Reiterate action and/or thank.

Your experiences working in the ID profession would be invaluable to me. Thank you for your time; I will call you next week.

Sincerely,

Kyle Hardeson

Requesting a letter of recommendation

Step 1: Request specific information or action.

Step 2: Cover relevant background and details.

Step 3: Provide contact information.

Step 4: Reiterate action and/or thank.

Alice Apple
100 Orchard Lane
Groves, Nebraska 12345

July 29, 2004

Della Johnson
39 North Ash Avenue
Swirling, Nebraska 12543

Dear Della,

Would you consider taking a moment to write a letter of recommendation on my behalf? I am applying for a position as a senior claims adjuster at Insurance Partners, and would be grateful for your recommendation.

The position for which I plan to apply requires specialization in fire, earthquake, and flood insurance; I would especially appreciate your tailoring your comments to highlight my experience in those areas.

Please call me if you need more information about the job or my request (333/399-7245). Address your letter to:

Alan Secure, Claims Manager
Insurance Partners
800 Office Park Boulevard
Swirling, Nebraska 12543

Your favorable recommendation should go a long way in helping me secure a job about which I'm very excited and confident I'll do well. Thank you for your confidence in my skills over the years and your willingness to help me succeed.

Sincerely,

Alice Apple

If you want the job, use Template 2

The majority of letters you'll write in this arena will probably be persuasive. You'll want your job application to stand out, to encourage someone to consider you. The best method for accomplishing this is a Template 2 letter.

Applying for an advertised job (application letter)

A top-notch application or cover letter does its best to match the applicant's need to those of the organization, the employer, and the position at hand. While your resume lists your qualifications, your cover letter makes explicit the match between those qualifications and the job requirements.

Step 1: Request specific information or action.

Step 2: State reasoning and relevant information.

Step 3: Stating or restating details needed for compliance isn't needed if you'll follow up.

Step 4: Reiterate request, demonstrating confidence.

Mr. Tom Windsong
2233 Walnut Lane
Pleasant View, New Jersey 00001
990-555-1234

February 4, 2004

Mr. Ed Simcox, Senior Recruiter
WXTV-TV
88 TV Boulevard
Metropolis, New York 11111

Dear Mr. Simcox:

Your ad in the January issue of the *National Sales Journal* stated your interest in an experienced ad sales representative. I am eager to join WXTV-TV in this capacity and am certain you'll find I have the qualifications you are seeking.

Among the qualifications I can offer WXTV-TV are:

Six years' experience in radio ad sales with WFFQ in Dallas, Texas. Consistently met or exceeded established sales quotas.

Proven ability to deal with corporate decision-makers. I am on the board of two local business associations and regularly work with corporate executives to plan civic fund-raising events.

Outstanding communication skills. I am an active member of Toastmasters and have made numerous presentations to my local chamber of commerce.

My resume is enclosed. I am anxious to explore the opportunity to join your experienced sales staff. Unless I hear from you before, I will call you within a week to discuss the next step.

Thanks for your consideration, and I will call you next week.

Sincerely,

Tom Windsong

Resume enclosed

Applying for a job with no posted vacancy (job query)

Step 1: Request specific information or action.

Step 2: State reasoning and relevant information.

Step 3: Stating or restating details needed for compliance isn't necessary if you'll follow up.

Step 4: Reiterate request, demonstrating confidence.

Julie Robinson
1 S. Broadway Avenue
St. Lawrence, Missouri 63333-1111
990/550-4765

January 23, 2004

Human Resources Director
Medco Pharmaceuticals
18 Medical Way
St. Lawrence, Missouri 63333-8888

Dear Human Resources Director:

Medco Pharmaceuticals needs qualified consultant pharmacists to ensure that their doctor, nurse, and healthcare facility customers use drugs wisely and responsibly. With eight years of experience in pharmacy consulting, I have the skills you seek. I would like to arrange for an interview in which to elaborate on my skills and demonstrate how Medco would benefit by bringing me on board!

The specific contributions I can make to Medco include:

- **Experience:** Consulted in nursing homes and other medical facilities throughout Missouri since 1990.
- **Innovation:** Developed a state-wide vaccination program that dramatically reduced facilities' long-term pharmaceutical costs and improved patient health.
- **Problem-solving:** Worked with minimal supervision in stressful and ever-changing health care environments.

My resume is enclosed. I will call you next week to see if we might arrange for a brief meeting at your convenience.

Thank you for your time, and I look forward to speaking with you next week.

Sincerely yours,

Julie Robinson

Enclosure

Applying for a first job or reentry into the job market

New graduates and individuals returning to work can use the design of Template 2 to strengthen their image as qualified job candidates. Use Step 2 to demonstrate to a potential employer that you've done your homework and that you understand the employer's business.

Ian Anders
2201 Cherrytree Lane
Whirling, Nebraska 12435
(321) 765-4321

June 28, 2004

Mark Kinders, Claims Supervisor
Protect-All Insurance
1 Tornado Lane
Swirling, Nebraska 12543

Dear Mr. Kinders:

Step 1: Request specific information or action.

Your senior claims adjuster Anna Smith informs me that Protect-All Insurance is seeking a programmer/analyst to develop and support new client/server applications in your claims division. I have the skills you're looking for and would like to request an interview.

Step 2: State reasoning and relevant information.

Using current and future computer technologies is one strategy Protect-All Insurance has always used to provide outstanding service to its policyholders. With my recent degree in integrated computer technologies from the Chamberlain Business School and experience working with a relational database and client/server applications, I offer you state-of-the-art know-how with complex network systems.

Step 3: Stating or restating details needed for compliance isn't needed if you'll follow up.

I offer you:
- Experience with Windows NT/XP, Linux.
- Experience with multiple servers.
- Outstanding interpersonal communications skills.
- Exceptional diagnostic skills.

Commit to taking follow-up action yourself versus waiting for the employer to call you!

Step 4: Reiterate request, demonstrating confidence.

I will call your secretary next week to see if we might arrange an interview at a convenient time. Thank you for your consideration.

Sincerely,

Ian Anders

Resume enclosed

Thanking for a job interview

Because the best reason to write a thank-you letter following a job interview is to continue to persuade this potential employer to hire you, treat these letters as persuasive letters. Thanking your interviewer is a second, slightly less important, purpose for these letters.

A first name is appropriate as you met in the interview.

Step 1: Request specific information or action.

End your first paragraph with a persuasive statement to give it primary emphasis.

Step 2: State reasoning and relevant information.

Following up on one specific selling point from your interview is an effective approach to continuing the persuasion.

Step 3: Stating or restating details needed for compliance isn't needed if you'll follow up.

Step 4: Reiterate request, demonstrating confidence.

Julie Robinson
1 S. Broadway Avenue
St. Lawrence, Missouri 63333-1111
990/550-4765

February 15, 2004

Nora Morton
Medco Pharmaceuticals
18 Medical Way
St. Lawrence, Missouri 63333-8888

Dear Nora:

Thank you for the interview on February 14. After speaking with you at length about Medco Pharmaceuticals' needs, I am completely confident I can fill the consultant pharmacist position currently available.

During our interview, I mentioned a vaccination program I conceptualized and implemented for a large healthcare client. A report I just received indicates a 28-percent drop in this client's quarterly pharmaceutical costs as compared to costs during the same period last year. The facility's administrator is convinced this program is chiefly responsible for the drop in costs.

I would love to speak to you further about introducing your clients to such a program. I will call your assistant, Ethan Gray, next week to see where you are in your interviewing process and see if we might arrange another meeting to continue our discussion.

Sincerely yours,

Julie Robinson

Providing an enthusiastic letter of recommendation

The more enthusiastic recommendation letters are actually persuasive in nature. They say, in essence, "I believe in this person's abilities enough to encourage you to consider him or her for this position." Letters slightly less enthusiastic can be handled with Template 4.

Step 1: Request specific information or action.

Step 2: State reasoning and relevant information.

Step 3: Stating or restating details needed for compliance isn't needed if you're not expecting follow-up contact.

Step 4: Reiterate request, demonstrating confidence.

Della Johnson
39 North Ash Avenue
Swirling, Nebraska 12543

August 3, 2004

Alan Secure, Claims Manager
Insurance Partners
800 Office Park Boulevard
Swirling, Nebraska 12543

Dear Alan Secure:

Alice Apple would make an outstanding senior claims adjuster at Insurance Partners, and I would encourage you to seriously consider her for the position.

I first met Alice when she came to Protect-All Insurance as a new claims adjuster. She reported directly to me for the first two years of her tenure with that company, from which I retired in 1996. In the four years I've followed Alice's career, I've watched her become one of the most knowledgeable problem-solvers in the company. For the last three years, she has handled fire, earthquake, and flood insurance almost exclusively.

In my professional opinion, Alice is ready for more responsibility and challenge in her profession than the smaller Protect-All Insurance can offer her. I feel confident Alice will be the asset to you that she has been to my colleagues and me for several years.

Yours truly,

Della Johnson
Former Claims Manager
(retired)

cc: Alice Apple

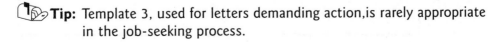 **Tip:** Template 3, used for letters demanding action, is rarely appropriate in the job-seeking process.

Use Template 4 to simply provide information

When you need to provide information and a persuasive approach isn't appropriate, use a letter based on Template 4.

Tip: You may be tempted to use Template 4 to voice a complaint to an employer. But if your key objective is getting your employer to right a wrong, Template 2 (persuading someone to take action) will be more effective.

Providing a letter of recommendation

If you do not feel comfortable writing a persuasive recommendation letter (perhaps you feel you don't know the individual's skills well or cannot fully recommend them), try Template 4 instead. A Template 4 letter reports the facts about your association with the recommendee but stops short of attempting to persuade.

An effective generic salutation identifies the recipient according to a role, such as "Prospective Employer."

Step 1: Overview information or event letter will address.

Step 2: Provide information or describe event. *Handle any less-than-ideal opinions with tact and objectivity.*

Step 3: Inviting recipient to contact you and providing contact information isn't appropriate if you do not expect follow-up contact.

Step 4: End with a lasting impression.

Irene Iverson
999 Clean Street
Tidy, Iowa 98765

September 17, 2004

Dear Prospective Employer:

Terry Mathews has provided housecleaning services for my family for the last year, and we have been pleased with her work.

Terry's responsibilities have included weekly routine cleaning of all rooms: dusting furniture, floors, and woodwork; vacuuming rugs; damp-mopping hardwood floors; and cleaning and sanitizing two bathrooms and a large kitchen. Occasionally she has also helped out with dishes, laundry, and even windows.

In my experience, Terry has always been responsive to any concerns raised, trustworthy, and reliable.

Sincerely,

Irene Iverson

Accepting a position

Step 1: Overview information or event letter will address.

Step 2: Provide information or describe event.

Step 3: Invite recipient to contact you; provide contact information.

An occasional one-line paragraph in the middle of a letter helps that information stand out.

Step 4: End with a lasting impression.

Ian Anders
2201 Cherrytree Lane
Whirling, Nebraska 12435
(321) 765-4321

August 15, 2004

Mark Kinders, Claims Supervisor
Protect-All Insurance
1 Tornado Lane
Swirling, Nebraska 12543

Dear Mark,

To follow up on our last conversation, I formally accept the programmer/analyst position we have been discussing.

Enclosed are signed copies of the confidentiality agreement and salary contract, at your request. I wrote in and initialed one small change on the contract, a change we discussed last week; if you have any questions about this change, please call me to discuss it.

Otherwise, I will report to your human resources department Monday morning, August 31.

Thank you, again, for demonstrating confidence in me; I'm eager to begin working with you and look forward to helping you take Protect-All Insurance into the next phase of its technological growth.

Sincerely,

Ian Anders

Enclosures: confidentiality agreement and salary contract

Tip: Need to reject a job offer instead? Because you'll probably want to preserve a relationship with those offering you the job, use Template 6. (See page 109.)

Tip: Should you respond to a rejection letter? Yes! Use Template 5. (See page 107.)

Acknowledging events or the receipt of information

Use Template 5 to acknowledge events or the receipt of information, whether that information is good news or bad news.

Thanking for informational interview or recommendation letter

Use Template 5 to acknowledge receiving someone's kindness in the form of an informational interview or a letter of recommendation, for instance. Thank-you letters for job interviews are different, however. (See the Tip that follows.)

Step 1: Acknowledge information or event.

A specific follow-up comment here increases the sincerity of your thank you.

Step 2: Elaborate as appropriate.

Step 3: End with a lasting impression.

Kyle Hardeson
6775 Bricklane Place
Alexandria, Virginia 65432-1256

April 18, 2004

Ms. Ellen Taylor, Instructional Designer
Performance Training Systems
100 Government Avenue
Washington, D.C. 76543

Dear Ellen:

Thank you for meeting with me to discuss instructional design and share your experiences with me. I found our discussion extremely valuable, and I was also impressed with the instructional design projects Performance Training Systems has undertaken.

Your information and advice helped me to decide to apply for that instructional design position at Applied Technologies. I won't know anything about how my interviews went for weeks, but I believe I have a pretty good shot at the position.

You and others have also encouraged me to pursue that Instructional Systems Technologies degree. As I mentioned to you, I'm a little overwhelmed at the prospect of returning to school; I am, however, committed to looking into it further.

Again, thanks for your encouragement and helpful suggestions.

Kind regards,

Kyle Hardeson

 Tip: Thank-you letters following job interviews should be treated as persuasive (Template 2) letters. While one purpose for such a letter should be, in fact, to thank your interviewer, your more important purpose is to continue persuading this potential employer to hire you! (See page 102.)

Responding to a rejection

When you've been turned down for a job, a thank-you letter is still warranted and the best approach to bowing out with dignity. Never handle such a letter with anger. You never know when an opportunity could lead you this employer's way again.

Step 1: Acknowledge information or event.

Step 2: Elaborate as appropriate.

Step 3: End with a lasting impression.

Mr. Tom Windsong
2233 Walnut Lane
Pleasant View, New Jersey 00001

March 19, 2004

Mr. Ed Simcox, Senior Recruiter
WXTV-TV
88 TV Boulevard
Metropolis, New York 11111

Dear Ed:

I received your letter informing me you had offered the ad sales representative position to another candidate. Thank you for letting me know of your decision so promptly.

Thank you, too, for taking the time to meet with me. I enjoyed our discussions and found them valuable regardless of their outcome for me.

Perhaps our paths will cross again in the future. Best of luck to you and WXTV-TV.

Sincerely,

Tom Windsong

 Tip: You might also respond to a rejection letter by requesting, in your letter, feedback about why you weren't offered the job. Instead of requesting the employer write you a letter providing this information, though, which would require more work from the employer, mention that you would like to call for this feedback (and be sure to do so!). Position your request as seeking "feedback to improve how I present my skills in the future."

To tactfully deliver bad news, use Template 6

Preserving a long-standing relationship, even when you must say no or deliver other bad news requires a Template 6 letter. Template 6 "softens" bad news.

Declining to provide a letter of recommendation

Step 1: Make general statement or restate request.

Step 2: Provide rationale behind negative response or bad news.

Step 3: State the negative response or bad news.

Step 4: An apology is not necessary here.

Step 5: End on a positive or encouraging note.

Derrick Sayles
8 Elm Avenue
Pleasant View, New Jersey 00001

April 3, 2004

Mr. Tom Windsong
2233 Walnut Lane
Pleasant View, New Jersey 00001

Dear Tom:

I was flattered to receive your call last week requesting a letter of recommendation.

Your skills as an ad sales representative are, I'm sure, very strong. Our association, of course, has been as board members for our local Speakers Association of America chapter. In this capacity I could certainly vouch for your skills in the art of persuasion.

Yet we haven't always agreed on board issues; most recently, our views on what fees we should pay local speakers could not be more different. In light of especially this recent issue, I worry that I could not provide a letter that displays no evidence of our conflict.

The bottom line, Tom, is that I believe you'd be better served to request such a letter from someone with whom you are not currently experiencing such a difference of opinion.

Good luck to you in your job search.

Sincerely,

Derrick Sayles

Declining a position

Julie Robinson
1 S. Broadway Avenue
St. Lawrence, Missouri 63333-1111
990/550-4765

March 16, 2004

Nora Morton
Medco Pharmaceuticals
18 Medical Way
St. Lawrence, Missouri 63333-8888

Dear Nora:

Step 1: Make general statement or restate request.

Thank you for your offer of the consultant pharmacist position. I especially appreciate the sincere effort you've made to become familiar with my skills and experience as we've tried to establish whether or not we have a "fit" between job and candidate.

Step 2: Provide rationale behind negative response or bad news.

The position is attractive to me because it seems to offer a lot of freedom in innovating and promoting new drug-monitoring and use programs. As I indicated in our last interview, however, I was disappointed to learn that Medco would not be in a position to reimburse tuition costs for my ongoing study toward a Doctor of Pharmacy degree, currently a primary professional goal of mine.

Step 3: State the negative response or bad news.

On March 14, I was offered another position by a company whose benefits package includes tuition reimbursement. Because I expect these costs to be substantial in the next two years, I have decided to accept this position.

Step 4: An apology is not necessary here.

I sincerely appreciate the time you have taken and the special inquiries you've made on my behalf during this interview process.

Step 5: End on a positive or encouraging note.

Thank you again for your consideration,

Julie Robinson

Resigning on favorable terms

No matter what the circumstances of a resignation, resignation letters should be positive, formal, and brief.

Step 1: Make general statement or restate request.

Step 2: Provide rationale behind negative response or bad news.

Step 3: State the negative response or bad news.

Step 4: An apology is not necessary here.

Step 5: End on a positive or encouraging note.

Julie Robinson
1 S. Broadway Avenue
St. Lawrence, Missouri 63333-1111

March 17, 2004

Wayne Lloyd, General Manager
RXV Pharmaceuticals
11 Pharmacy Way
St. Lawrence, Missouri 63333-9999

Dear Wayne:

My three-year tenure at Jones and Sons, now RXV Pharmaceuticals, has been the most challenging and rewarding period of my career, and I regret having to make a difficult announcement.

With the buyout last quarter of Jones and Sons Pharmaceuticals by RXV and possible future layoffs of consultant pharmacists, I have felt compelled to explore outside job possibilities.

As a result, I've recently accepted another position and must inform you that effective March 31, 2004, I will be resigning from RXV Pharmaceuticals.

Both you and my associates at Jones and Sons have taught me a lot; what's more, I've come to regard those I work most closely with as almost a second family. I will truly be sorry to go.

I hope you can understand my decision to leave RXV.

Yours truly,

Julie Robinson

Resigning on less-than-favorable terms

Even in adverse circumstances, a resignation letter must remain professional. This letter will likely be your last formal contact with the organization; you're best served to leave the best possible lasting impression.

Rehashing the adverse circumstances behind your resignation would be senseless at this point. Instead, think of your letter's purpose as announcing your intentions and your resignation's effective date. As a courtesy, you may choose to explain your reason for resigning—but explain briefly, tactfully, *blamelessly*, and only if doing so will not bring professional repercussions.

Step 3: State the negative response or bad news. If your resignation should come as no surprise, you may choose to start with your point, the resignation, which reorganizes your steps.

Step 2: Provide rationale behind negative response or bad news. **Option 1:** Include your reason *tactfully*. **Option 2:** Omit your reason (not necessary when the boss knows why you're resigning).

Especially when leaving under adverse circumstances, briefly *stating a key accomplishment can help document your contribution to the organization.*

Step 4: No apology is necessary here.

Step 5: End on a positive or encouraging note.

Alice Apple
100 Orchard Lane
Groves, Nebraska 12345

August 13, 2004

Paige Conner
Protect-All Insurance
1 Tornado Lane
Swirling, Nebraska 12543

Dear Paige,

Recent events demand that I resign from Protect-All Insurance, effective August 31, 2004.

My disagreement with the intent of several claim-filing policies—as well as their inconsistent application—has prevented me from performing my job effectively.

My experience at Protect-All Insurance has taught me much, and I am grateful for the experience. I am especially proud of achieving the "senior" claims adjuster title after just one year of consistently exceeding all quality and production goals.

I appreciate having had the opportunity to work with so many talented and terrific people. I wish all of you the best.

Sincerely,

Alice Apple

Post-Secondary School Admissions Letters

Handle any letter you send to or about a school as a business communication, rather than a social one. A concise, well-written letter can give school officials the best possible impression of you, demonstrate how you think and communicate, and suggest how you are likely to perform at the school. A professionally written letter can also help someone providing a reference to write a more effective one.

School admissions letter samples

Use Template 1 for information requests

If your goal is to request general information about admissions, financial aid, grade transcripts, and the like, use Template 1.

Requesting school application or admission requirements or financial aid information

To ensure that you get the information you need, state your request as soon as possible and make sure you're specific about exactly what you need.

Step 1:
Request specific information or action.

Step 2:
Cover relevant background and details.

Step 3:
Provide contact information.

Step 4:
Reiterate action and/or thank.

Mark Harris
22 Bubbling Brook Lane
Hot Springs, Arkansas 46576

January 3, 2004

Admissions Officer
Southeastern College
37977 Academic Avenue
Seaside, Georgia 85555

Dear Admissions Officer:

Please send me an application for admission to Southeastern College, a current catalog, and, if available, a fall schedule of classes. I'd also be grateful for any information you can provide (or advice on whom to write or call for information) about:

- Financial aid.
- Grants or loans.
- Scholarships.

I will graduate from Hot Springs High School this May and am interested in possibly starting at Southeastern in the fall. I plan to double major in journalism and telecommunications.

If you have questions about my request, please call me at 522/667-3221.

Thank you for your assistance, and I look forward to receiving this information.

Sincerely,

Mark Harris

Requesting an informational interview or tour

Mark Harris
22 Bubbling Brook Lane
Hot Springs, Arkansas 46576

February 28, 2004

Gene Wallace
Admissions Officer
Southeastern College
37977 Academic Avenue
Seaside, Georgia 85555

Dear Mr. Wallace:

Step 1:
Request specific information or action.

My parents and I will be visiting Southeastern College March 20, 21, and 22. Could you arrange to have someone meet with us to answer some of our questions about Southeastern and perhaps also guide us on a tour of the campus?

Step 2:
Cover relevant background and details.

I'm most interested in seeing the journalism, telecommunications, and broadcasting areas and in finding out especially what kinds of advanced technologies I would be learning to use as a student there. I'd greatly appreciate any time someone could make available to us any of these three days.

I have narrowed my school choices to three, and a closer look at the campus could really help me determine if Southeastern would be the right choice for me.

Step 3:
Provide contact information.

Please write or call to let me know if you can help us. My phone number is 522/667-3221.

Step 4:
Reiterate action and/or thank.

Thank you for your assistance, and perhaps I'll have the opportunity to meet you in March!

Sincerely,

Mark Harris

Requesting a letter of reference

Step 1:
Request specific information or action.

Step 2:
Cover relevant background and details.

Step 3:
Provide contact information.

Step 4:
Reiterate action and/or thank.

Mark Harris
22 Bubbling Brook Lane
Hot Springs, Arkansas 46576

March 15, 2004

Mr. Abraham Issacs
Hot Springs High School
1101 Rockwalk Row
Hot Springs, Arkansas 46576

Dear Mr. Issacs:

Would you be willing to write a letter of reference to help me obtain a scholarship? Southeastern College offers eight $2,500 Future Leaders scholarships annually, and I believe I may be eligible to receive one.

The scholarships will be awarded to those who best demonstrate both academic excellence and leadership skills. As both my journalism teacher and faculty advisor of the *Hot Springs Times*, you're in a unique position to offer a perspective on my abilities in both areas.

The school must receive all scholarship materials by May 1. For your convenience, I've enclosed a stamped envelope addressed to the school's scholarship administrator. If I can provide more information about the scholarship, please let me know.

With my brother already in his second year at college, my family will really be able to use a Future Leaders scholarship. Thank you for helping me with a letter of reference.

Sincerely,

Mark Harris

Requesting a copy of a transcript

Paula Avery
89 Windblown Lane
Ocean View, Maine 21211

October 11, 2004

Office of the Registrar
Great Hope College
Meadow Way
Clearing, Oklahoma 61548

Dear Registrar Official:

Step 1: Request specific information or action.

Please send me three copies of my grade transcript. I have enclosed a check for $15 to cover the cost of this service.

Step 2: Cover relevant background and details.

My student ID is 399-39-3997. I was a student at Great Hope from August 1992 to May 1996 and was graduated with a B.S. in education.

I understand that my request may take up to three weeks to fulfill. Because potential employers are already asking me for this information, I would greatly appreciate receiving the transcripts sooner than three weeks (if possible).

Step 3: Provide contact information.

If you have questions about my request, please call me at 207/555-7667.

Step 4: Reiterate action and/or thank.

Thank you for your assistance.

Sincerely,

Paula Avery

To be persuasive, use Template 2

Requests that are other-than-routine and situations calling for a persuasive approach call for Template 2.

Providing a letter of reference

Step 1: Request specific information or action.

Step 2: State reasoning and relevant information.

Step 3: Stating or restating details needed for compliance isn't necessary if you're not expecting follow-up contact.

Step 4: Reiterate request, demonstrating confidence.

Mr. Abraham Issacs
Hot Springs High School
1101 Rockwalk Row
Hot Springs, Arkansas 46576

March 30, 2004

Ms. Cynthia Brandywine, Scholarship Administrator
Southeastern College
37977 Academic Avenue
Seaside, Georgia 85555

Dear Ms. Brandywine:

Mark Harris is an outstanding candidate for a Future Leaders scholarship, and I highly recommend him for your consideration.

Mark has been in my English, journalism, and photography classes for the past three years at Hot Springs High School. As both his teacher and the faculty advisor for the *Hot Springs Times*, for which he has served as editor during his junior and senior years, I can attest to both his academic excellence and his leadership skills.

Mark is a straight-A student who also assumes primary responsibility for getting our weekly publication out on schedule. On occasion, this has meant rallying his editorial staff to work late into the evening to reach a publication deadline.

Mark seems especially talented at recognizing the skills of individual staff members and enhancing those skills by assigning, and then coaching, staff members to succeed with appropriate tasks. Last semester he recognized the talents of one very shy photographer who now heads our photography team. Mark's coaching made the difference for this student, as it has for so many others who have served on the *Hot Springs Times* editorial staff.

I feel confident Mark will do well at Southeastern College, and a Future Leaders scholarship would help his family to help him succeed.

Sincerely,

Abraham Issacs
Hot Springs High School

117

👉 **Tip:** Template 3, used for letters demanding action, is rarely appropriate when you're applying for school admission.

Using Template 4

When a persuasive approach isn't needed, but you still need to provide information, use Template 4.

Accepting attendance

Step 1: Overview information or event letter will address.

Step 2: Provide information or describe event.

Step 3: Invite recipient to contact you and provide contact information.

Step 4: End with a lasting impression.

Mark Harris
22 Bubbling Brook Lane
Hot Springs, Arkansas 46576

May 15, 2004

Gene Wallace and the Admissions Committee
Southeastern College
37977 Academic Avenue
Seaside, Georgia 85555

Dear Mr. Wallace and the Admissions Committee:

I was delighted to receive your letter notifying me that Southeastern has accepted me as an entering student for fall 2004. I do, indeed, plan to attend.

Enclosed is the information you requested about my housing needs and financial aid arrangements to date.

If you need further information, please call me at 522/667-3221. I understand I'll be receiving additional information this summer about what to expect this fall.

I'm eager to begin my college career at Southeastern.

Sincerely,

Mark Harris

Enclosure: completed admissions packet

Acknowledging events or the receipt of information

Use Template 5 to acknowledge events or the receipt of information, whether that information is good news or bad.

Thanking for a letter of reference

Step 1: Acknowledge information or event.

Step 2: Elaborate as appropriate.

Step 3: End with a lasting impression.

Mark Harris
22 Bubbling Brook Lane
Hot Springs, Arkansas 46576

May 28, 2004

Mr. Abraham Issacs
Hot Springs High School
1101 Rockwalk Row
Hot Springs, Arkansas 46576

Dear Mr. Issacs:

I got a Future Leaders scholarship!

No doubt your letter was influential in the college's decision. Thank you for agreeing to provide a letter of reference.

I can't tell you how much you've helped me, both academically and personally, over the past few years. I'll never forget you, Mr. Issacs.

Thanks again,

Mark Harris

Thanking for an informational interview

Mark Harris
22 Bubbling Brook Lane
Hot Springs, Arkansas 46576

April 1, 2004

Mr. Gene Wallace
Admissions Officer
Southeastern College
37977 Academic Avenue
Seaside, Georgia 85555

Dear Mr. Wallace:

Thank you for meeting with my parents and me Saturday, March 21.

We found your information and Ms. Anderson's very thorough tour most helpful in allowing me to get a feel for what attending Southeastern will be like. Southeastern is definitely a top choice for me at this point.

I look forward to hearing from your admissions committee about my application. Thank you, again, for taking time on a Saturday to help both me and my family to make this important decision.

Yours truly,

Mark Harris

Step 1: Acknowledge information or event.

Step 2: Elaborate as appropriate.

Step 3: End with a lasting impression.

To tactfully deliver bad news, use Template 6

Preserving a long-standing relationship, even when you must say no or deliver other bad news, requires a Template 6 letter. Template 6 "softens" bad news.

Declining to provide a letter of reference

Ms. Erica Wainsmythe
Hot Springs High School
1101 Rockwalk Row
Hot Springs, Arkansas 46576

March 19, 2004

Mark Harris
22 Bubbling Brook Lane
Hot Springs, Arkansas 46576

Step 1: Make general statement or restate request.

Dear Mark:

I was flattered to receive your letter this week requesting a letter of reference for a Future Leaders scholarship.

Step 2: Provide rationale behind negative response or bad news.

As your physics teacher, I can certainly attest to your academic abilities: Your grades in my class have consistently been As and Bs.

Step 3: State the negative response or bad news.

Step 4: An apology is not necessary here.

I don't feel, though, that I'm in the best position to provide information on your leadership skills. This semester is the first semester I've had you in class. Teachers talk among themselves, of course; and you are spoken of as a leader among your peers. But I would encourage you to request a reference letter from those teachers with whom you've had the most opportunity to demonstrate those skills. (Have you approached Mr. Isaacs or Miss Jamison?)

Step 5: End on a positive or encouraging note.

I'm sure many teachers would be both willing and better-suited to provide letters for you. If I can help talk to those teachers on your behalf, I would be happy to. Good luck to you with your scholarship.

Sincerely,

Ms. Wainsmythe

Declining attendance

Step 1: Make general statement or restate request.

Step 2: Provide rationale behind negative response or bad news.

Step 3: State the negative response or bad news.

As a courtesy, a brief, honest explanation might be appropriate.

Step 4: An apology is not necessary here.

Step 5: End on a positive or encouraging note.

Mark Harris
22 Bubbling Brook Lane
Hot Springs, Arkansas 46576

May 22, 2004

Mr. Eric Adams
Admissions Officer
Great Hope College
Meadow Way
Clearing, Oklahoma 61548

Dear Mr. Adams:

I was pleased to receive your letter notifying me that Great Hope has accepted me as an entering student for fall 2004.

While Great Hope would be relatively close to home for me, and I respect the school's religious tradition, I felt I needed to seriously consider whether its journalism, telecommunications, and broadcasting departments would offer me access to state-of-the-art production technologies. Exposure to these will ultimately give me a competitive edge in my job search.

I have decided, therefore, to attend Southeastern College this fall. I was impressed with the advanced technologies that seem to be more available at a larger school.

I appreciate the time you took to help us become familiar with Great Hope. Thank you again for your consideration.

Sincerely,

Mark Harris

Parent-School
Letters

Communicating with a teacher, coach, or school official by letter tends to suggest that your message is more official or formal than a message communicated face to face or by telephone. Keep your letter friendly, yet brief and to the point.

Parent-school letter samples

Use Template 1 to request information or action

Use Template 1 to formally request information or make a routine request.

Requesting information

Doris Mackey
1102 Plains Road
Wheatshaft, Kansas 25625

October 6, 2004

Mr. Herman Voight
Grover Middle School
8678 Grain Grove
Wheatshaft, Kansas 25625

Dear Mr. Voight:

Step 1: Request specific information or action.

Before giving our permission for Philip to attend the October 15 field trip to the Children's Museum and Arcade World, please answer a few questions for my husband and me:

- What is the purpose of this day-long field trip?

Step 2: Cover relevant background and details.

- What specific programs will the children be required to attend while at the museum?
- How many adults will be accompanying the class?
- Will the children have English class assignments related to this trip?
- If Philip does not attend this field trip, how will he be spending his English period, and who will supervise his activities?
- What—specifically—is the purpose of the Arcade World excursion?

Step 3: Provide contact information.

Please call me by Tuesday of next week to answer our questions. My office number is 555-2020; our home number is 555-1245.

Step 4: Reiterate action and/or thank.

Thank you for taking the time to answer my questions.

Sincerely,

Doris Mackey

An alternative to complaining: Requesting information

Step 1: Request specific information or action.

Step 2: Cover relevant background and details.

Step 3: Provide contact information.

Step 4: Reiterate action and/or thank.

Doris Mackey
1102 Plains Road
Wheatshaft, Kansas 25625

November 11, 2004

Phyllis Mathews, Principal
Grover Middle School
8678 Grain Grove
Wheatshaft, Kansas 25625

Dear Ms. Mathews:

I'm hoping that you can help me understand the reason why my son, Philip Mackey, seems to be spending an overabundance of his English class time this semester participating in what appear to be nonacademic activities.

Over the past six weeks, for instance, Philip has spent five or six English classes watching videos, generally action films such as *Speed* and *Die Hard*. He never seems to have assignments relating to the films and cannot tell me why entire class periods are spent in this way.

Philip has mentioned several times that his regular English teacher, Herman Voight, has often been absent and that substitute teachers almost never seem prepared to lead the group in productive academic activities. I understand they often simply leave the room while the children are either entertained by a video or given a "study hall" free period.

I have left several messages requesting to arrange a conference with Mr. Voight but have had no response over several weeks.

I would appreciate a call from you or Mr. Voight within the next two weeks with information about the purpose for and the extent of these nonacademic activities. Please call me at my office (555-2020) or at home evenings (555-1245).

I would appreciate your prompt attention to what I consider a serious problem, especially with a student for whom English is not a strong subject.

Sincerely,

Doris Mackey

cc: Herman Voight

Requesting a conference with a teacher

Lou Carroll
Rural Route 6
Great Lakes, Michigan 76654

March 3, 2004

Norman Underwood
Great Lakes High School
42 Abbott Drive
Great Lakes, Michigan 76654

Dear Mr. Underwood:

Step 1: Request specific information or action.

My wife, Janice, and I have seen a marked decrease in our daughter, Noreen's, performance in your algebra class during the last two grade periods. We'd like to make an appointment with you to discuss your ideas on what might be causing the problem and how we might work with you to help her.

Step 2: Cover relevant background and details.

Mrs. Hamilton in the main office tells me that your regular conference period runs from 3:30 p.m. to 4:30 p.m. on Tuesdays, Wednesdays, and Thursdays. Would it be possible to meet with you next Wednesday, March 11, at 4 p.m.?

Step 3: Provide contact information.

Please leave a message on our home answering machine confirming this day or suggesting an alternative. Because my wife's work regularly takes her out of town during the day, 4 p.m. would be the earliest time we both could meet you.

Our number is 968-9696.

Step 4: Reiterate action and/or thank.

We'll wait to hear from you. Thank you for taking the time to meet so we may work together to help Noreen succeed.

Sincerely,

Lou Carroll

For less-than-routine requests, use Template 2

Use Template 2 for requests that are unusual, beyond routine, or likely to get resistance. The best approach to complaining is to instead request action.

Requesting a change of teacher or class

Step 1: Request specific information or action.

Step 2: State reasoning and relevant information.

Step 3: State or restate details needed for compliance.

In a difficult situation, use a firm, confident— but never confrontational— tone.

Step 4: Reiterate request, demonstrating confidence.

Doris Mackey
1102 Plains Road
Wheatshaft, Kansas 25625

December 11, 2004

Phyllis Mathews, Principal
Grover Middle School
8678 Grain Grove
Wheatshaft, Kansas 25625

Dear Ms. Mathews:

In keeping with our recent discussions, please transfer my son, Philip Mackey, to another English class for the rest of the school year.

Philip needs solid attention in English, and I do not feel his current teacher or curriculum offers this. Typically a "C" writer, Phil has consistently received A's this semester, but he receives virtually no writing assignments! And assignments requiring command of grammar, always a difficult area for Phil, receive only pass/fail grades and minimal feedback.

Furthermore, my husband and I have been particularly troubled by what continues to be an obvious lack of academic rigor in Mr. Voight's classroom. Consider the following:

- Extensive class time viewing entertainment videos with no educational purpose and no corresponding assignments.
- Recently, a day-long class trip (which included a visit to Arcade World) with, again, minimal or no educational value.
- Mr. Voight's extensive absences from class, which result in substitute teachers consistently unprepared to teach.
- Mr. Voight's unwillingness to address my concerns, which I've presented to him by telephone, in person, and by letter.

I would be willing to see Phil transferred to either of the other two sections of this class. Both teachers seem quite competent and their lesson plans, academically sound. The change should be effective January 4, 1999.

Thank you for your cooperation in this matter. I look forward to hearing from you by semester's end with your decision.

Thank you,

Doris Mackey

cc: Herman Voight

Tip: Template 3, used for letters demanding action, is rarely worth alienating teachers or parents (and quite probably affecting their relationship with your child as well). If a Template 1 or Template 2 letter fails to yield results, your best bet may be to take your requests to a third party, for instance, a school board. For such letters, use Template 4.

When persuasion isn't necessary

Use Template 4 to provide information when a persuasive approach isn't needed.

Explaining child's absence from class

Step 1: Overview information or event letter will address.

Step 2: Provide information or describe event.

Step 3: Invite recipient to contact you. (Contact information isn't necessary if the recipient already knows how to contact you.)

Step 4: End with a lasting impression.

Lonnie Applegate
506 Sunblest Way
Rolling Hills, New Hampshire 76454

April 15, 2004

Donald Morgan
Jefferson Elementary School
11380 State Road 28
Rolling Hills, New Hampshire 76454

Dear Mr. Morgan:

Please excuse Tommy's absence from school the last two days. He's had a stomach flu and has been confined to bed since Monday morning. He was still a little shaky this morning but really wanted to return to school.

If Tommy has any trouble with his stomach today, please call me; I'll be home almost all day, and I could pick him up anytime.

One last thing: I understand that Tommy missed a math test yesterday. He's quite concerned about it, and I would appreciate your giving him extra time both to prepare for the test and to complete his other overdue assignments.

Thank you,

Lonnie Applegate

Excusing child from an activity

Because the decision to give or deny permission for an activity lies with the parent, handle excuse letters with Template 4.

Step 1: Overview information or event letter will address.

Step 2: Provide information or describe event.

In sensitive situations, always tell a teacher how much your child knows about this letter and how you expect the teacher to handle the information: "Please do not mention this letter to Jimmy," or "Jill is aware of my concerns, so please feel free to discuss this issue with her."

Step 3: Invite recipient to contact you and provide contact information.

Step 4: End with a lasting impression.

Doris Mackey
1102 Plains Road
Wheatshaft, Kansas 25625

October 13, 2004

Mr. Herman Voight
Grover Middle School
8678 Grain Grove
Wheatshaft, Kansas 25625

Dear Mr. Voight:

Philip Mackey will not be attending the day-long field trip on Thursday, October 15, to the Children's Museum and Arcade World.

As you know, my husband and I have been concerned about Philip's performance in both his English and social studies classes. As much as we hate to prevent Phil from enjoying the day with his friends, we strongly feel that such activities will not help him improve academically and that academics, in fact, currently need to be his focus.

We've explained our feelings to Phil, and he is prepared to spend his English period studying. I understand that your colleague Joy Adams will be available during this period to both supervise his activities and help him with a social studies report on which he's currently working.

If you need further information about our request, please call me at 555-2020 (office) or 555-1245 (home).

Phil's father and I are very proud of how Phil is handling this situation. One last concern we share with him is the possibility his classmates may view his absence from the field trip as some sort of punishment. Phil has decided to tell his friends that he, in fact, needs the time to finish his report and is taking his parents' advice to "pass" on the trip. We would, finally, appreciate your publicly supporting Phil in putting academics first this time.

Thank you for your assistance on this important matter,

Doris Mackey

Declaring your intention to go to the school board

If you've decided to take your concern to a third party, and you are not seeking a response from the original party, inform that individual of your actions with a Template 4 letter.

Step 1: Overview information or event letter will address.

Step 2: Because previous letters fully described the problem, it is not necessary to describe event. Simply attach copies of these letters.

Step 3: Inviting recipient to contact you and providing contact information isn't appropriate if you do not expect follow-up contact.

Step 4: End with a lasting impression.

Doris Mackey
1102 Plains Road
Wheatshaft, Kansas 25625

January 11, 2005

Phyllis Mathews, Principal
Grover Middle School
8678 Grain Grove
Wheatshaft, Kansas 25625

Dear Ms. Mathews:

Because my son, Philip Mackey, must continue to tolerate an English class and teacher who has consistently demonstrated a lack of academic rigor, I will be taking my concerns to the Grover County School Board.

Copies of my previous letters (attached) detail my concerns about Mr. Voight and his lack of even the most basic attention to my son's educational needs.

I regret having to take my concerns to the school board. However, I consider the current situation intolerable, and my son's education requires that I take this next step.

Principal Mathews, I understand that often a school principal's hands are tied from taking needed action; nonetheless, I appreciate the ongoing attention you've given to my concerns even if you have not been able to act on them.

Sincerely,

Doris Mackey

Attachments: copies of previous letters
Copy: Herman Voight

 Tip: To gracefully end a long-standing relationship with a teacher, coach, or principal, use Template 6 instead to "soften" the bad news.

Addressing a concern to the school board

Doris Mackey
1102 Plains Road
Wheatshaft, Kansas 25625

January 11, 2005

Dr. James Davidson
President, Grover County School Board
P.O. Box 575
Wheatshaft, Kansas 25625

Dear Dr. Davidson:

Step 1: Overview information or event letter will address.

I have encountered a serious, ongoing problem involving the quality of my son's English class and the lack of academic rigor employed by its instructor, Mr. Herman Voight. Because ongoing discussions with both the teacher and Principal Mathews have failed to either improve the class or get my son moved to another class, I am appealing to you and the board for immediate assistance.

Step 2: Provide information or describe event.

Copies of my letters to both Mr. Voight and Principal Mathews, dated from October 2004 to January 2005, along with their responses if I received them, are attached.

Step 3: Invite recipient to contact you and provide contact information.

Please call me for any additional information I can provide about this situation: 555-2020 (office) or 555-1245 (home).

As each day goes by without action, my son—not to mention the others in his class—continues to be denied the quality of language education I know is possible in this school system. I hope you will decide to take quick action.

Step 4: End with a lasting impression.

I will call you in two weeks (unless I've heard from you beforehand) to learn what our next step should be.

Thank you for your assistance,

Doris Mackey

Attachments: copies of previous letters
Copies: Phyllis Mathews, Principal, Grover Middle School
Herman Voight, Teacher of 6th Grade English

To show appreciation, use Template 5

Template 5 is appropriate for acknowledging someone's act of kindness or display of outstanding service.

Expressing appreciation to a teacher or coach

Step 1:
Acknowledge information or event.

Step 2:
Elaborate as appropriate.

A one-sentence paragraph gives particular emphasis to that sentence.

Step 3: End with a lasting impression.

Lou and Janice Carroll
Rural Route 6
Great Lakes, Michigan 76654

May 12, 2004

Norman Underwood
Great Lakes High School
42 Abbott Drive
Great Lakes, Michigan 76654

Dear Mr. Underwood:

We greatly appreciate the extra attention you've given our daughter, Noreen, this semester. You've had such an effect on her!

Not only have her grades shown improvement, but her self-esteem has as well. As you know, this was the first time in Noreen's academic career that math gave her difficulty. Before you began tutoring her after school, she was spending three to four hours every evening doing math homework, yet her grades continued to fall. When anyone in the family had tried to help her, she simply became more frustrated and impatient with us—and with herself.

With your assistance, Noreen has regained her confidence, and her math homework has again become manageable (for all of us).

Math may present future challenges for our daughter as she begins college in the fall, but she's approaching next year without fear, thanks to you.

Gratefully,

Lou and Janice Carroll

c: Charles Regent, Principal

To tactfully deliver bad news, use Template 6

Preserving a long-standing relationship with a teacher, coach, or principal even when you must say no or deliver bad news requires a Template 6 letter. Template 6 "softens" bad news.

Tip: If your bad news will not come as a big surprise or you aren't concerned about maintaining a long-standing relationship, get to the point more quickly with Template 4.

Withdrawing a child from school

Step 1: Make general statement or restate request.

Step 2: Provide rationale behind negative response or bad news.

Step 3: State the negative response or bad news.

Step 4: An apology is not necessary here.

Step 5: End on a positive or encouraging note.

Doris Mackey
1102 Plains Road
Wheatshaft, Kansas 25625

May 21, 2004

Phyllis Mathews, Principal
Grover Middle School
8678 Grain Grove
Wheatshaft, Kansas 25625

Dear Ms. Mathews:

As you know, I've had regular, ongoing concerns about the quality of my son, Philip's, English class.

Throughout the school year, I've expressed these concerns to you and, at your suggestion, to the Grover County School Board. Both you and the board have been sympathetic but, unfortunately, unwilling to either move my son to another class or replace his teacher.

Effective in the fall, Philip will no longer be attending Grover Middle School. We've decided he needs special attention in English and have therefore decided to enroll him in a private school.

Thank you again for the time you've taken to listen to my concerns.

Sincerely,

Doris Mackey

Consumer Letters and
E-mails

With an occasional exception, most consumer letters and e-mails are written to get action and often to right a wrong (a defective product, a product in need of repair, unfair treatment, and so on).

Consumer experts don't always agree on the best approach to get the results you seek when you have a complaint, but they offer lots of good advice. Here's a sampling of what some experts suggest (thanks to the research of John Bear, Ph.D., author of *Send This Jerk the Bedbug Letter*):

Regarding your letter's first impression:

📧 First impressions are important. Use good paper and type or computer print the letter. Never use handwriting. (Patricia H. Westheimer and Jim Mastro, *How to Write Complaint Letters That Work*)

📧 Be businesslike. Don't use stationery with flowers or little animals in the corners. (Anthony Joseph, *Christian Science Monitor*, "Contact the Right People")

📧 Make it easy for the business to get in touch. Professional stationery may add clout. (Joe Dziemianowicz, *McCalls*, "How to Write a Complaint Letter That Gets Results")

📧 A neat and tidy letter improves the chance of a reply. (Ruth Nauss Stingely, *Reader's Digest*, "It Pays to Complain")

Regarding your letter's tone:

📧 Address your letter to a real person. An actual name is essential. How do *you* like getting letters addressed to "Occupant" or "To whom it may concern"? (Patricia H. Westheimer and Jim Mastro, *How to Write Complaint Letters That Work*)

📧 Establish rapport. Point out (if true) that you have been a loyal customer, that you admire the organization. (Ruth Nauss Stingely, *Reader's Digest*, "It Pays to Complain")

- Begin your letter with a genuine compliment if possible. (Joe Dziemianowicz, *McCalls*, "How to Write a Complaint Letter That Gets Results")

- The tone of a letter is important. Try to be "calm, but not apologetic...firm but not hostile." (American Association of Retired Persons, *How to Write a Wrong, Complain Effectively, and Get Results*)

- Be firm and businesslike. Don't scream on paper. (David Horowitz, *Fight Back and Don't Get Ripped Off*)

- Don't write when you are angry. (Ruth Nauss Stingely, *Reader's Digest*, "It Pays to Complain")

- Be firm, but not angry. (Anthony Joseph, *Christian Science Monitor*, "Contact the Right People")

- Be firm but courteous. (Joe Dziemianowicz, *McCalls*, "How to Write a Complaint Letter That Gets Results")

- Speak firmly; be explicit about what you want. (Stephen A. Newman and Nancy Kramer, *Getting What You Deserve: A Handbook for the Assertive Consumer*)

- Many people become indignant and defensive when threatened. Companies are the same. (Patricia H. Westheimer and Jim Mastro, *How to Write Complaint Letters That Work*)

- Be subtle. Don't make threats; don't promise dire consequences or a lawsuit. (Morris J. Bloomstein, *Consumer's Guide to Fighting Back*)

- End the letter positively. Invite them to phone you. (Ruth Nauss Stingely, *Reader's Digest*, "It Pays to Complain")

Regarding who should receive your letter:

- Never talk to anyone without authority or who won't give you his or her name and title. When you write, choose the lowest-level person who seems authorized to help. (Stephen A. Newman and Nancy Kramer, *Getting What You Deserve: A Handbook for the Assertive Consumer*)

- Reach the right person from the start. Phone first to determine who the right person is. "To speak with someone without authority is to waste your breath and beg for a brush-off." (Morris J. Bloomstein, *Consumer's Guide to Fighting Back*)

- Send it to someone with power. Don't mark it "personal, confidential." (David Horowitz, *Fight Back and Don't Get Ripped Off*)

- Consider writing to the consumer relations department first; save the president for a later offensive. (Anthony Joseph, *Christian Science Monitor*, "Contact the Right People")

- Always write to an officer, by name; always write to the national headquarters, not to a local or regional office. (Anthony Joseph, *Christian Science Monitor*, "Contact the Right People")

- Write to the person in charge by name: either the president or someone lower with a copy to the president. (Ruth Nauss Stingely, *Reader's Digest*, "It Pays to Complain")

- Address your complaint to the president. (Joe Dziemianowicz, *McCalls*, "How to Write a Complaint Letter That Gets Results")

- Write to the top: the owner, president, or chairperson. Send a copy to managers who may be more responsible; and if they act quickly, they will look better to their bosses. (Patricia H. Westheimer and Jim Mastro, *How to Write Complaint Letters That Work*)

- If the letter doesn't work, go right to the "blockbuster": a repeat of the last letter with copies to the manufacturer, the Better Business Bureau, the chamber of commerce, your member of Congress, the Office of Consumer Affairs, Consumers Union, and a newspaper or radio action line. (Morris J. Bloomstein, *Consumer's Guide to Fighting Back*)

Regarding your letter's length:

- Be brief but be thorough. (American Association of Retired Persons, *How to Write a Wrong, Complain Effectively, and Get Results*)

- Get to the point quickly. (David Horowitz, *Fight Back and Don't Get Ripped Off*)

- Don't ramble. Never write more than one page. (Joe Dziemianowicz, *McCalls*, "How to Write a Complaint Letter That Gets Results")

- Be short. (Ruth Nauss Stingely, *Reader's Digest*, "It Pays to Complain")

Regarding what your letter should include:

- Be sure you have your facts straight. (Stephen A. Newman and Nancy Kramer, *Getting What You Deserve: A Handbook for the Assertive Consumer*)

- Be specific. Tell exactly what happened. If products are involved, give the model and serial number. Enclose copies of your proof of purchase. Make clear how the problem affected you. (Joe Dziemianowicz, *McCalls*, "How to Write a Complaint Letter That Gets Results")

- State clearly what you want the company to do, and set a deadline. (Joe Dziemianowicz, *McCalls*, "How to Write a Complaint Letter That Gets Results")

- Make a clear demand; show proof of your claim; quote a law or statute; don't mention or bring in third-party agencies until the second letter. Don't carbon the world; the company will be turned off because you didn't give them a chance. (David Horowitz, *Fight Back and Don't Get Ripped Off*)

- Indicate your intention of going to public agencies, small claims court, trade associations, action lines, or newspapers or magazines where the seller advertises. Companies may be impressed by your knowledge and intentions. (Stephen A. Newman and Nancy Kramer, *Getting What You Deserve: A Handbook for the Assertive Consumer*)

Regarding setting a response deadline:

- Act as if your time were valuable. Give deadlines. (Stephen A. Newman and Nancy Kramer, *Getting What You Deserve: A Handbook for the Assertive Consumer*)

- Set a time limit for a reply. Two weeks is fair. (David Horowitz, *Fight Back and Don't Get Ripped Off*)

- Allow three to four weeks for response. (Anthony Joseph, *Christian Science Monitor*, "Contact the Right People")

And when you get no reply:

- Try a "write, call, write" sequence. Wait 10 days; then call. If you can't get through, write a stronger second letter with a copy of the first enclosed. (Patricia H. Westheimer and Jim Mastro, *How to Write Complaint Letters That Work*)

- If you get no response, send one more letter with a clear deadline. If that doesn't work, go to third parties. (Joe Dziemianowicz, *McCalls*, "How to Write a Complaint Letter That Gets Results")

- Escalate quickly. Set short deadlines for a response before you go to a higher lever. Ten days is reasonable. (Stephen A. Newman and Nancy Kramer, *Getting What You Deserve: A Handbook for the Assertive Consumer*)

- If you receive no reply in four to six weeks, try again; if you receive no satisfaction then, go to third parties. If you do get satisfactory results, send a thank-you letter. (Ruth Nauss Stingely, *Reader's Digest*, "It Pays to Complain")

Consumer letter samples

For straightforward requests, use Template 1

Requesting information or routine action from a company, making a reservation, placing an order, or making a straightforward return: These everyday transactions you may have as a consumer call for a Template 1 letter.

Making a reservation

The more straightforward the request, the shorter the letter can be. Reservation letters are generally brief and to the point.

Step 1: Request specific information or action.

Step 2: Cover relevant background and details.

Step 3: Provide contact information.

Step 4: Reiterate action and/or thank.

Grace Nelson
1884 46th Avenue
Karden, New Jersey 98755-4321

January 4, 2004

Juliette Merriman
Arlott's Lodge
1802 Scenic Way
Pine Grove, North Carolina 11223-4556

Dear Ms. Merriman:

Will you please reserve a double room for my husband and me for Friday, February 6 through Sunday, February 8?

We plan to arrive before 6 p.m. Friday evening. I understand that you do not need a credit card to hold our reservation so long as we arrive before 6 p.m. If you have questions about my request, please call me: (999) 555-4009.

Please confirm our reservation by January 12. Thank you.

Sincerely,

Grace Nelson

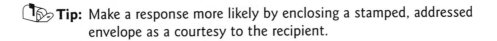 **Tip:** Make a response more likely by enclosing a stamped, addressed envelope as a courtesy to the recipient.

Requesting information from a merchant

To ensure that you get the information you need, make sure you're specific about exactly what that is.

Francine Andrews
744 Sledding Lane
Burr, Minnesota 55443

January 2, 2004

Customer Service Representative
Copymate Incorporated
707 Duplication Way
Atlantis, Georgia 55555

Dear Customer Service Representative:

Step 1: Request specific information or action.

Please send me information and literature on midprice copiers appropriate for my home office.

These are the features I'm looking for:

Step 2: Cover relevant background and details.

- Copy speed at least 10 pages per minute.
- Copy surface large enough for 11 1/2" x 14" documents.
- Multiple paper trays.
- Enlarging capabilities to 200 percent.
- Reduction capabilities to 50 percent.
- Collating and stapling capabilities.
- Easy toner replacement (ideally a cartridge versus a roller).

I am writing to several companies for information and will make a purchase in the next month based on the information I receive. Please include copier prices, as well as details and fees for any maintenance plans you offer.

Step 3: Provide contact information.

Please do not have a sales representative contact me. However, if you have questions about my request, call me at 990/555-1009.

Step 4: Reiterate action and/ or thank.

Thank you for your assistance, and I look forward to receiving this information.

Sincerely,

Francine Andrews

Requesting information from a utility

Tara Wilcox
608 Coverdale Drive
Maplehill, Louisiana 54245
980/555-3039

March 7, 2004

Residential Phone Service Representative
South-Central Phone Company
203 Bell Drive North
Maplehill, Louisiana 54245

Dear Phone Service Representative:

Step 1: Request specific information or action.

Could you please provide me with a detailed listing of all charges above the monthly base rate ($25.85) now due on phone number 990/555-3039?

Step 2: Cover relevant background and details.

My roommate, Betty J. Anderson, recently moved out of our apartment, and we'd like to split our utility expenses before she leaves the country in three weeks.

You should have received our February payment of $68.82. But because you bill any additional charges one month in arrears, we need a detailed listing of any additional charges we incurred from February 10 through March 5 (Betty's actual move-out date).

Step 3: Provide contact information.

Step 4: Reiterate action and/ or thank.

Please write or call me with this information before March 28. I appreciate your prompt response; your help will ensure that you receive prompt, full payment on our account.

Sincerely,

Tara Wilcox

Placing an order for merchandise or service

Ordering something without an order form requires that your information be complete. Otherwise, you're bound to get something you didn't want!

Tom Graison
7003 Flowerfield Way
Bloomton, West Virginia 35353-0110

August 1, 2004

Reference: Customer ID 0123 78901

Sales Representative
The Dutch Touch
P.O. Box 3055
Bulbtown, Illinois 61677-3055

Attention: Sales Department

Dear Sales Representative:

Step 1:
Request specific information or action.

Please send me the following bulbs from your summer sale catalog.

S7893 24 Mixed Giant Crocus @ $ 8.99	=	$ 8.99
S8882 16 Giant Jonquils @ $10.99	=	10.99
S9770 10 White Narcissus @ $13.99	=	13.99
S0299 20 Pink Daffodil Mixed @ $19.99	=	19.99
S1022 2 Royal Red Amaryllis @ $ 8.99 **ea**.	=	17.98
Subtotal		$71.94
Shipping & Handling		11.50
(Using chart in your catalog)		
Total		$83.44

Step 2:
Cover relevant background and details.

Step 3:
Provide contact information.

I've enclosed a check for $83.44. If you have any questions about my order or if you anticipate any shipping delay, please call me at 123/555-1011.

Step 4:
Reiterate action and/or thank.

Thank you for your usual prompt handling of my order; unless I hear otherwise, I look forward to receiving my bulbs within the next three to four weeks.

Sincerely,

Tom Graison

Following up on an order for merchandise or service

Okay, you've placed your order, but nothing happened. A follow-up phone call or letter is in order. To avoid offending anyone, handle this first follow-up not as a complaint, but as a request for information. If your follow-up doesn't work, a Template 3 and/or Template 4 letter could be your next step.

Step 1: Request specific information or action.

Step 2: Cover relevant background and details.

Step 3: Provide contact information.

Step 4: Reiterate action and/or thank.

Tom Graison
7003 Flowerfield Way
Bloomton, West Virginia 35353-0110

September 10, 2004

Reference: Customer ID 0123 78901

Customer Service Representative
The Dutch Touch
P.O. Box 3055
Bulbtown, Illinois 61677-3055

Attention: Customer Service Manager

Dear Customer Service Representative:

Did you receive my August 1 bulb order? I haven't received my bulbs and am concerned that we may have a problem.

These were the bulbs I expected to receive no later than last week:

S7893 24 Mixed Giant Crocus @ $ 8.99	=	$ 8.99
S8882 16 Giant Jonquils @ $10.99	=	10.99
S9770 10 White Narcissus @ $13.99	=	13.99
S0299 20 Pink Daffodil Mixed @ $19.99	=	19.99
S1022 2 Royal Red Amaryllis @ $ 8.99 **ea**.	=	17.98

In my letter I asked you to call me with any questions or anticipated delays (123/555-1011). I received no such call. I enclosed a check with my order for $83.44 ($71.94 plus $11.50 shipping & handling).

Please send my order immediately or call me within the next 10 days to explain its status. I am concerned but feel confident that you'll handle this situation with your usual outstanding service.

Sincerely,

Tom Graison

143

An alternative to complaining: Requesting information on a rent increase or maintenance problem

Brett Tenant
65 Pinegrove Court
Jefferson, Virginia 51244

October 1, 2004

Maryann Landlord
88 Pinegrove Hill
Jefferson, Virginia 51244

Dear Maryann Landlord:

Step 1: Request specific information or action.

Your letter explaining the increase in my rent raised some questions for me; could you please answer them?

Step 2: Cover relevant background and details.

1. As you know, when I moved in three years ago, I was told my rent would not go up every year. Are you aware that it has?

Rent November 1995:	$425
Rent as of October 1996:	$480
Rent as of November 1997:	$510
Rent proposed November 2004:	$530

2. Are you also aware that my rent has increased nearly 25% since I moved in?

3. Are you aware that comparable apartments in this area rent more in the range of $400–$480?

4. Finally, when might I expect the next increase, and are you willing to guarantee no increase before that time?

Step 3: Provide contact information.

Step 4: Reiterate action and/ or thank.

Please drop me a note or call me (555-8293) with answers to these questions. I'd appreciate hearing from you before my November rent payment is due.

Sincerely,

Brett Tenant

Canceling an order for merchandise or service

Handle straightforward cancellations briefly, but be sure to include all information the provider will need to accommodate your request.

Step 1: Request specific information or action.

Step 2: Cover relevant background and details.

Step 3: Provide contact information.

Step 4: Reiterate action and/or thank.

Alvin Artesan
5099 Workingman's Way
Clinton, Georgia 65656

April 5, 2004

Reference: Customer Account Number 00017592

Customer Service Representative
Residential Delivery
The Clinton Daily Times
One Times Plaza
Clinton, Georgia 65656

Attention: Residential Delivery Manager

Dear Customer Service Representative:

Please stop delivery of *The Clinton Daily Times* to my home effective immediately.

My wife and I have enjoyed receiving your publication for years. Unfortunately, our jobs now have us both traveling most weeks, and we simply cannot keep up with a daily paper.

I believe we have prepaid for April; please send us a refund for the issues we will not receive. If you have questions about this cancellation request, please leave a message at (199) 555-5612, and either my wife or I will call you back as soon as we can.

Thank you for years of reliable delivery of a top-notch newspaper. If our situation changes, we'll call you to resume delivery. In the meantime, we'll expect delivery to stop no later than the end of this week.

Sincerely yours,

Alvin Artesan

Returning merchandise

Straightforward returns, too, can make for short letters. How much of an explanation you include is up to you. Be clear, however, about whether you're seeking an exchange or refund.

Step 1: Request specific information or action.

Step 2: Cover relevant background and details.

Step 3: Provide contact information.

Step 4: Reiterate action and/or thank.

Rhonda Walter
383 Mountain View Lane
Plains, Wyoming 66455

December 5, 2004

Reference: Customer ID 10728-3920

Customer Service Representative
Johnson Gifts
10 Alexandria Boulevard
Charming, North Carolina 87881

Attention: Customer Service Manager

Dear Customer Service Representative:

Enclosed is the Auto Lock De-Icer I received by mail two weeks ago. I'd like a refund for this product because it does not suit my needs.

Your catalog seemed to describe a device that was exactly what I've needed for door locks that continually freeze throughout the winter. And the small heated metal rod seemed a more environmentally sound solution than those disposable tubes of alcohol I'd been using.

But this flimsy device falls into pieces when I try to install the batteries. Couldn't such a device be better made so it won't fall apart in my hands (let alone in a coat pocket, where I'd need to keep it)? If you offer such a device, I'd love to hear about it (111/555-3993).

As for this device, however, I expect a full refund—including my cost to ship it back to you. Copies of both my sales receipt and a receipt for return postage are enclosed. Please send me my refund within the next two weeks.

Thank you,

Rhonda Walter

Requesting return of a deposit

When you are clearly entitled to the return of a deposit, a simple, short request should be all that's required. But if you anticipate any disagreement about whether you're entitled to the return, Template 2 (persuading others to take action) would be more appropriate.

Step 1: Request specific information or action.

Step 2: Cover relevant background and details.

Step 3: Provide contact information.

Step 4: Reiterate action and/or thank.

Frank Eagletree
888 Sandybeach Way
Flamingo, Florida 10501

July 2, 2004

Marianne Baxter, Owner
The Bare Earth Shoes
75 Vistana Avenue
Seagull, Florida 10462

Dear Marianne Baxter:

Please return the $20 deposit I left with you for the Ecosound shoes you ordered for me two weeks ago. (Enclosed is my receipt for the deposit.)

When you called last week to tell me your distributor could not get the shoes for six to eight weeks, I checked around here in Flamingo and was able to find a pair immediately.

In case my number isn't handy and you have any questions, it's 499/555-3092.

Thank you for checking into this for me—and especially for letting me know you were experiencing a delay. You still have the best prices in Florida for Earth-friendly shoes. You can bet I'll shop with you again.

Sincerely,

Frank Eagletree

Requesting repair or replacement (under warranty)

When your defective product or poor quality service is covered by a warranty or return policy of some kind, a simple request for a repair or replacement—or even a refund—should get the results you seek.

Step 1: Request specific information or action.

Step 2: Cover relevant background and details.

Step 3: Provide contact information.

Step 4: Reiterate action and/or thank.

Jason Young
87 Canyon View Drive
Santa Oceana, California 92126-1010

October 11, 2004

Ted Sunshine, President
Glare-free, Inc.
100 Clear Vision Road
Santa Oceana, California 92126

Dear Mr. Sunshine:

Please replace the enclosed pair of defective sunglasses.

I purchased these glasses from your shop four months ago. As you can see, the color is already wearing off the metal frames.

Enclosed with the sunglasses is a copy of my sales receipt. If you have questions or concerns about my request, I can be reached at 599/555-4335.

Thank you for your understanding and prompt response.

Sincerely,

Jason Young

For consumer complaints, use Template 2

Requests that are unusual, beyond routine, or likely to run into resistance call for Template 2. The best approach to complaining is to instead request action.

Requesting repair or replacement (no longer under warranty)

If Jason Young's sunglasses were no longer covered under warranty but he nonetheless felt they should be repaired without cost, his request would be less-than-routine. A more persuasive letter would be more effective.

Step 1: Request specific information or action.

Step 2: State reasoning and relevant information.

Step 3: State or restate details needed for compliance.

Step 4: Reiterate request, demonstrating confidence.

Jason Young
87 Canyon View Drive
Santa Oceana, California 92126-1010

July 11, 1999

Ted Sunshine, President
Glare-free, Inc.
100 Clear Vision Road
Santa Oceana, California 92126

Dear Mr. Sunshine:

Please repair or replace the enclosed pair of defective sunglasses.

I purchased these glasses from your shop just over one year ago. While they are no longer under warranty, you can see that the color is wearing off the metal frames.

These are not inexpensive sunglasses, and I certainly did not expect them to show such wear in just a year's time. They receive no unusually harsh treatment; in fact, when I'm not wearing them, I *always* store them in their case. Shouldn't a quality pair of sunglasses show wear better than these are showing?

Enclosed with the sunglasses is a copy of my sales receipt. I do not feel I should be charged for a repair or replacement. If you have questions or concerns about my request, I can be reached at 599/555-4335.

My preference would be to receive a replacement pair unless you can assure me that a repair will really solve the problem. I do not want to be writing you again in a few months.

Thank you for your understanding in this matter. I've purchased sunglasses from your company for years, and I feel certain you'll make this right.

Sincerely,

Jason Young

Requesting a refund

Wanda Wardrobe
1 Buena Vista Lane
Bonita, California 34388

November 13, 2004

Reference: Customer Account 4072 38809

Customer Service Representative
Best Dressed Catalog Fashions
301 Fashion Lane
Fenton, Massachusetts 69654

Dear Customer Service Representative:

Please refund my purchase price and return postage cost for the enclosed blouse.

I've also enclosed a copy of my sales receipt. Although you'll find I purchased this blouse more than two months ago, I only recently experienced a problem with it when I washed it for the first time. It fell apart!

Your clothes are generally very high quality. I am quite surprised at the how poorly this blouse seems to have been made. In fact, I was somewhat afraid to wash it at all, but I liked the look of the blouse so much, I decided to keep it. When I did wash it, I followed the washing instructions on the label to the letter. If you have any questions about my handling of the blouse, please call me: (211) 555-3902.

Is this an indication of the quality I can expect from Best Dressed Catalog Fashions in the future?

Because I paid for the blouse by check, I would appreciate your returning my purchase price, $39.99, along with the my postage cost (postage receipt also enclosed) by check as well.

Thank you for your prompt handling of my return.

Yours truly,

Wanda Wardrobe

Informing utility of a billing error

Toby Spring
Rural Route 104-C
Pleasant, Ohio 21222

April 12, 2004

Customer Service Representative
Federated Gas Companies
10 South Main Street
Pleasant, Ohio 21212

Dear Customer Service Representative:

Step 1: Request specific information or action.

I need your help in resolving what must be a billing error on my March bill.

Step 2: State reasoning and relevant information.

My average monthly bill for wintertime gas usage runs $80.40. With the unusually warm weather we've had in February and March, my family has actually turned our heat off for weeks at a time during these months.

How, then, could our March gas bill be $115.80?!

Step 3: State or restate details needed for compliance.

Please call or write me with either a revised amount due or a detailed explanation for these charges before this bill's due date, April 28. My phone number is 990/555-8729.

Step 4: Reiterate request, demonstrating confidence.

I look forward to hearing from you within the next two weeks.

Sincerely yours,

Toby Spring

Breaking a service contract

Eliot Templeton
66885 Twisted Oak Parkway
Pathway, Oregon 78855
555/984-7321

December 1, 2004

Reference: Account 10 0472 80938

Rick LeMasters, Customer Service Representative
Easy Access Internet
23 Transistor Way
Pathway, Oregon 78855

Dear Rick:

Please cancel my service contract and refund the monthly fee I've paid for the past three months.

As we discussed on the telephone yesterday, I've had virtually no opportunity to take advantage of your service given repeated busy signals and the apparently limited ability of our modems to communicate. Your usage records can confirm that I've been able to use your service perhaps a half dozen times over the past three months.

I understand that you typically do not refund customers' monthly fees beyond the trial period (the first month after sign-up) or in situations in which they've used the service at all during a given month; however, I'm sure you'll agree that my circumstances are unique. I have, in fact, been prevented from using the service I've been paying for.

Please call me at the phone number I've listed above with any questions or concerns about my request. I will expect the automatic billing through my local phone company to end with my next month's bill. Please send my refund check to my home address (above).

Thank you for your cooperation and understanding in this matter.

Regards,

Eliot Templeton

Breaking a lease; requesting security deposit return

Brett Tenant
65 Pinegrove Court
Jefferson, Virginia 51244

November 1, 2004

Maryann Landlord
88 Pinegrove Hill
Jefferson, Virginia 51244

Dear Maryann Landlord:

Step 1: Request specific information or action.

I will be moving out December 1, 2004, and request that my security deposit, $425, be returned to me at that time.

Step 2: State reasoning and relevant information.

As you're already aware, I've had concerns about regular rent increases resulting in a monthly rent now well beyond that for comparable apartments in this area. Since we spoke on October 13, I understand your inability to provide me with a guarantee that my rent won't continue to go up. Unfortunately, I simply cannot afford such increases.

I'm sure you'll agree I've been a model tenant for the past three years; I can also assure you that the apartment is in terrific shape—better shape, in fact, than when I moved in, given the landscaping improvements I've made over the years.

Step 3: State or restate details needed for compliance.

I plan to vacate the apartment on December 1 and would appreciate receiving my returned deposit as close to that date as possible. In fact, could I pick it up from you that afternoon?

Step 4: Reiterate request, demonstrating confidence.

Thank you for your understanding of my situation. I will call you in the next week to find out when I might receive my security deposit.

Sincerely,

Brett Tenant

Another alternative to complaining: Requesting help

If you're thinking of sending a complaint letter and you haven't yet decided what would make things right, instead of zeroing in on the problem in an emotion-packed way, make your goal to persuade someone to work the problem out with you.

Step 1: Request specific information or action.

Step 2: State reasoning and relevant information.

Morton Hamilton
Rural Route 1908
Farmington, Nebraska 43363

April 27, 2004

Technical Services Manager
Technocomm, Inc.
84 Business Machine Way
Commuting, Nebraska 43364

Dear Technical Services Manager:

I need your help with a situation I'm finding increasingly frustrating.

Approximately six months ago, I purchased your top-of-the-line plain paper fax machine Model 600Q. This model's features clearly make it one of the best machines on the market.

But here's my dilemma. I've had endless difficulties getting help in using even the machine's most basic features (for instance, redialing, speed dialing, and broadcast faxing). Here's a synopsis of the trouble I've experienced:

- Instructions in the owner's manual are very difficult to follow.
- Calls for technical support have kept me holding 20 to 30 minutes!
- Your voice-mail system has disconnected me numerous times, generally after these long waits.
- The technicians I finally reach offer ample advice without fully understanding my difficulties.
- Their quick answers—and unwillingness to remain on the line while I try their advice—invariably do not solve my problem.

Step 3: State or restate details needed for compliance.

- I'm faced with starting all over with another long wait, another technician, and a machine I still cannot use.

Please call me within the next couple of weeks with your advice: (899) 555-0114.

Step 4: Reiterate request, demonstrating confidence.

I was willing to pay more for Technocomm's quality. Now what can I do to get your organization's help in using my machine?

Thank you,

Morton Hamilton

Informing of hazardous product

Although this letter's purpose is, in part, to inform a company of a potentially dangerous problem you've experienced with its product, your overriding purpose is probably to attempt to convince the company to do something about the problem. So treat this as a persuasive letter.

Aaron Moran
9 Baily Terrace
Pikesville, Connecticut 12121
(112) 889-4990

June 17, 2004

Paul J. Priestman, President
Kiddie Komfort Furniture
10 Tykes Way
Boomer, Colorado 21212

Dear Mr. Priestman:

Subject: Dangerous product!

Step 1: Request specific information or action.

My family has experienced what I'm sure you'll agree is a serious problem with one of your products. My sincere hope is that you will act to either fix this problem or remove this product from the market.

Step 2: State reasoning and relevant information.

The product is your Handy Gate safety gate, Model QL780, your only model (to my knowledge) with a spring-loaded handle that allows an adult to "open" the safety gate to pass through while leaving the gate still anchored in the doorway.

On three occasions over two months, my 22-pound toddler has pushed the gate over and gone tumbling over with it.

Fortunately, we keep the gate on a level surface, so her injuries were negligible. But I know people who use these gates to keep toddlers away from stairways and other uneven surfaces; a spill in these cases could be disastrous.

Step 3: Details needed for compliance were provided with the return address, including a phone number.

Rest assured, we've made every possible adjustment to keep the gate anchored in the doorway. We've spoken to your customer service representatives and even exchanged one gate for another, hoping our first one was simply defective; the second was no different.

Your company has graciously accepted our return of the gate. I would appreciate a response, by mail or telephone, to this letter.

Step 4: Reiterate request, demonstrating confidence.

I fully expect that you will look into this matter before a child is seriously hurt.

Yours truly,

Aaron Moran

If previous requests fail, try Template 3

Didn't get action from your Template 1 or Template 2 letter? A stronger letter may be warranted. Letters demanding action are most appropriate after two initial attempts, by phone or letter, have failed and a reasonable amount of time has passed.

Demanding action

When a follow-up letter is fruitless, you may opt to send a stronger letter. Use Template 3 to turn up the heat.

Step 1: State letter's purpose; acknowledge previous requests.

Step 2: Restate concern or request.

Step 3: State expectations and possibly next steps.

Step 4: State or restate details needed for compliance.

Step 5: Reiterate request and (optionally) thank.

Tom Graison
7003 Flowerfield Way
Bloomton, West Virginia 35353-0110

September 28, 2004

Reference: Customer ID 0123 78091

Ellen Kostman, Customer Service Manager
The Dutch Touch
P.O. Box 3055
Bulbtown, Illinois 61677-3055

Dear Ellen Kostman:

We apparently have a problem, and I need your assistance. This is the third letter I've sent your department regarding an order I placed nearly two months ago; in addition, no one I speak to by phone seems to have the authority to help me.

You cashed my check for $83.44 more than a month ago for bulbs I have not received. My order, once more, was for:

S7893 24 Mixed Giant Crocus @ $ 8.99	=	$ 8.99
S8882 16 Giant Jonquils @ $10.99	=	10.99
S9770 10 White Narcissus @ $13.99	=	13.99
S0299 20 Pink Daffodil Mixed @ $19.99	=	19.99
S1022 2 Royal Red Amaryllis @ $ 8.99 **ea.**	=	17.98

I expect to receive my order express mailed to me within the week. If I do not receive my order, I am prepared to lodge a formal complaint with the Bulbtown Chamber of Commerce and the Better Business Bureau. If you need to speak with me, my number is 123/555-1011.

I look forward to receiving my order within one week.

Sincerely,

Tom Graison

Attachments: copies of previous letters and canceled check

When to use Template 4

Use Template 4 letters to provide information a company requests from you or to state action you are taking. You may be tempted to use Template 4 to voice a complaint to a company. But if your key objective is getting the company to right a wrong, Template 2 (persuading someone to take action) will be more effective.

Declaring your intention to go to a third party

If you've chosen to take some definitive action, such as lodging a complaint with a third party or taking your business elsewhere, and you are not seeking a response from the original party, inform that individual or organization of your actions with a Template 4 letter.

Step 1: Overview information or event letter will address.

Step 2: Provide information or describe event. *Because previous letters fully described the problem, simply attach copies of these letters.*

Step 3: (Invite recipient to contact you and provide contact information) isn't appropriate if you do not expect follow-up contact.

Step 4: End with a lasting impression.

Tom Graison
7003 Flowerfield Way
Bloomton, West Virginia 35353-0110

October 7, 2004

Reference: Customer ID 0123 78091

Ellen Kostman, Customer Service Manager
The Dutch Touch
P.O. Box 3055
Bulbtown, Illinois 61677-3055

Dear Ellen Kostman:

Because I have not received a response to any of three previous letters I've sent you regarding an order I've paid for but never received (nor a satisfactory response from several phone calls), I will be taking my concerns to the Bulbtown Chamber of Commerce and the Better Business Bureau.

Copies of my previous letters are attached.

I regret having to take this action—particularly with a company from which I've purchased merchandise for years. However, I feel I have no other option.

Sincerely,

Tom Graison

Attachments: copies of previous letters and canceled check
cc: President, The Dutch Touch

Reporting to a third party

When you've come to the end of the line with a consumer problem, you could always consider small claims court. However, you might also want to describe the problem to any one of a number of agencies with influence in the business community: State Attorney General, chambers of commerce, trade associations, the Better Business Bureau, your member of Congress, Office of Consumer Affairs, Consumers Union, publications in which the company advertises, newspaper, or radio action lines.

Step 1: Overview information or event letter will address.

Step 2: Provide information or describe event.

Step 3: Invite recipient to contact you and provide contact information.

Step 4: End with a lasting impression.

Tom Graison
7003 Flowerfield Way
Bloomton, West Virginia 35353-0110

October 8, 2004

President, Bulbtown Chamber of Commerce
One Commerce Way
Bulbtown, Illinois 61677

Dear Chamber President:

I have received what I consider unusually poor service from a company in your area and felt that reporting the situation to your chamber was important. I'm sure you will share my concern about the unreasonable treatment I've received from this Bulbtown company.

Copies of my letters to this company, The Dutch Touch (P.O. Box 3055, Bulbtown, Illinois 61677-3055), dating from early August to early October, detailing my difficulties, are attached. My situation involves an $80 order for which I have paid and never received merchandise.

If I can provide you with more information or if you can be helpful to me in recouping my $80, please call me (123/555-1011).

Sincerely,

Tom Graison

Attachments: copies of previous letters and canceled check
cc: President, The Dutch Touch

To show appreciation, use Template 5

Template 5 is appropriate for acknowledging someone's act of kindness or display of outstanding service.

Recognizing good service

Morton Hamilton
Rural Route 1908
Farmington, Nebraska 43363

June 8, 2004

Technical Services Manager
Technocomm, Inc.
84 Business Machine Way
Commuting, Nebraska 43364

Dear Technical Services Manager:

Step 1: Acknowledge information or event.

Your technician, Ms. Sharon Almstadt, really helped me out of a frustrating situation, and I'd like to commend both her work and your company for the help I've received.

Step 2: Elaborate as appropriate.

I had purchased your top-of-the-line plain paper fax machine Model 600Q but was having endless difficulties getting help in using even the machine's most basic features. A copy of my original letter to you outlining my difficulties is attached.

Ms. Almstadt called me not once, but several times, to make sure I was getting the answers I needed to make my fax machine fully operational. On one occasion she spent more than an hour on the telephone with me—even staying beyond her normal work hours—to help me sort out a problem we eventually learned resulted more from a faulty phone line than from any deficiency with your product.

Step 3: End with a lasting impression.

If making talented technicians like Ms. Almstadt truly available to your customers is an indication of the service I can expect in the future, you can be sure I'll recommend Technocomm machines to all of my business associates.

Sincerely yours,

Morton Hamilton
Attachment

Tactfully take business elsewhere using Template 6

Most of us treat our relationships with companies more matter-of-factly than our relationships with individuals. If we decide to take our business elsewhere, for instance, we typically just say so (in a Template 4 letter) or just do it without saying so.

However, if you've had a long-standing relationship with a particular service provider, you may want to handle ending that relationship as a Template 6 letter. Template 6 "softens" bad news.

Ending a long-standing business relationship

In a salutation using someone's first name only, either a comma or colon is appropriate.

Step 1: Make general statement or restate request.

Step 2: Provide rationale behind negative response or bad news.

Step 3: State the negative response or bad news.

Step 4: Apologize, if warranted.

Step 5: End on a positive or encouraging note.

Sarah Tomlin
90098 Rolling Way
Dalton, Ohio 55644

October 3, 2004

Dana Sheers
Hair Extraordinaire
30 North Mane Street
Dalton, Ohio 55644

Dear Dana,

Your move to a new salon and change to working fewer hours—so you can pursue other career goals—sound exciting, and I'm happy for you.

Over the 15 years you've been my hairdresser, I've followed you from salon to salon, waited devotedly for you to return to hairdressing after an eight-month hiatus, and remained devoted as your availability has decreased (no doubt because you've been in greater and greater demand) and your prices, over time, have increased.

Unfortunately, your new far-Northside location, your change to working part-time hours, and your recent 20-percent price increase have made it necessary for me to find another hairdresser.

I'm sorry I won't be able to keep the appointment we set for next month; but I know you'll have no difficulty filling the slot.

Thank you for years of making me look good. You're a talented hairdresser, and I sincerely wish you the very best as your career (and personal) goals continue to evolve. Best wishes, too, to you and your fiancé.

Take care,

Sarah

Letters for Banking and Credit Concerns

The best way to handle many credit and banking situations is with a brief letter that expresses your point quickly and simply, yet still provides any details the letter's recipient needs to take necessary action. Emotion generally has no place in such letters; keep your tone factual and business-like.

Note that we advise you not to send e-mails about banking and credit concerns, in order to protect your secure account information.

Banking and credit letter samples

For straightforward requests, use Template 1

Requesting information or routine action from a bank, credit card company, or a creditor calls for a Template 1 letter. If your request is less than routine, and especially if you anticipate resistance, use Template 2 for a more persuasive approach.

Requesting a credit report

If you don't have a specific name, use a generic position title.

Step 1: Request specific information or action.

Step 2: Cover relevant background and details.

Step 3: Provide contact information.

Step 4: Reiterate action and/or thank.

Martin Langford
1 Rangeline Road
Rolling Ranch, TX 99989

November 12, 2004

Reference: Social Security Number 300-40-4509

Credit Bureau Representative
Federated Credit Services
500 North Michigan Avenue
Metropolis, New York 35645

Dear Credit Bureau Representative:

Could you please send me a copy of my current credit report?

On November 1, First America Bank recently denied my application for a Visa card, and I understand that I am entitled to receive, without charge, a copy of my credit report within 30 days of this denial.

If you need further information from me to provide this report, please call my home at 214/555-0398.

Thank you for your prompt attention to my request.

Sincerely,

Martin Langford

Adding or removing someone from a credit account

Step 1: Request specific information or action.

Step 2: Cover relevant background and details.

Step 3: Provide contact information.

Step 4: Reiterate action and/ or thank.

Timothy Mayhern
911 Rolling Rock Ridge
Mountain Valley, Montana 12123

October 25, 2004

Reference: Account Number 1212 600 4484 6131

Customer Service Representative
ChargeCard Cardholder Services
Second National Bank
Farfield, Vermont 65655

Dear Customer Service Representative:

Please add my son's name to my ChargeCard account, effective immediately, and provide him a card in his name.

My 18-year-old son, Thomas Mayhern, will begin school out of state in January, and I'd like him to have access to the family ChargeCard account.

Currently, this account has two cardholders, my wife, Judith, and me. Thomas would be the third cardholder.

Naturally, as primary cardholder, I retain primary responsibility for any charges incurred on this account. (Thomas should be using the card only for agreed-upon school expenses and for emergencies.)

If I can provide additional information about this request, please call me at (122) 555-9734. Otherwise, we'll be looking to receive an additional card in Thomas's name by mail sometime before January 1, 1999.

Sincerely,

Timothy Mayhern

Requesting information on available services

To ensure that you get the information you need, make sure you're specific about exactly what that information is.

If you don't have a specific name, use a generic position title.

Step 1: Request specific information or action.

Step 2: Cover relevant background and details.

Step 3: Provide contact information.

Step 4: Reiterate action and/or thank.

Ralph Everhardt
Rural Route 1514
Landmark, Idaho 45958

December 3, 2004

Bank Representative
First Federated State Bank
106 East Tenth Street
Garden Grove, Idaho 45889

Dear Bank Representative:

Please send me information about your bank's savings and checking accounts.

I will be moving to Garden Grove within the month and will be looking for a bank to which I can transfer my account balances.

These are the services I'm most interested in:

- No-fee checking when I maintain a minimum balance.
- Overdraft protection or automatic transfer from savings.
- Extended banking hours on Friday afternoons and Saturday mornings.
- No-fee, reliable 24-hour access to ATMs.
- ATMs conveniently located downtown and on the northwest side.
- No-fee telephone banking.
- Christmas Club or youth-oriented savings accounts.

Please be sure to include your complete fee schedule, hours of operation, and rules and regulations for these accounts.

If you have questions about my request, please call me at 208/555-4903.

Thank you for your assistance, and I look forward to receiving this information so that I may choose the bank that best meets my family's needs.

Sincerely,

Ralph Everhardt

Requesting status of a loan application

Step 1: Request specific information or action.

Step 2: Cover relevant background and details.

Listing key details in table form can make responding to your letter easier.

To tactfully give a response deadline, begin with your rationale for the deadline.

Step 3: Provide contact information.

Step 4: Reiterate action and/or thank.

Nadine Ireland
Rural Route 7017
Mission, Kansas 77414

April 3, 2004

Loan Officer Geraldine Hartman
First Mission Bank
35 Courthouse Circle
Mission, Kansas 77414

Dear Geraldine Hartman:

I seem to be having some difficulty determining the status of my pending loan. Can you assist me?

My husband and I met with you and applied for a small business loan more than three weeks ago. But we have yet to receive any further information about it. Where do we stand?

Borrowers' names and SSNs:	Alfred & Nadine Ireland
	312-87-8695 & 307-98-1242
Type of loan:	Standard Small Business
Loan amount:	$17,500
Application date:	March 18, 2004

Because our plans to build additional office space hinge on receiving this loan and we are already negotiating with contractors, please call us by the end of next week with any information you can provide. You may reach me on weekdays at 316/555-7878.

I would greatly appreciate any information or anything you can do to help speed up the processing of our loan. I look forward to hearing from you by the end of next week.

Sincerely,

Nadine Ireland

Instructing that an overpayment be applied to a mortgage principal

Step 1: Request specific information or action.

Step 2: Cover relevant background and details.

Step 3: Provide contact information.

Step 4: Reiterate action and/ or thank.

Benjamin Smith
15 North Royal Drive
Palace, Pennsylvania 79798

July 24, 2004

Mortgage Representative
First Mortgage Corporation
First Mortgage Way
Moneytree, Maine 45454

Dear Mortgage Representative:

Please apply the $201.48 overpayment I'm making this month to the principal of my mortgage loan.

Amount of July payment:	$1,000.00
Amount due:	798.52
Additional amount to be applied to principal	$ 201.48

Please call me with any concerns about how this overpayment should be applied: 880/555-1810.

Thank you for your usual efficient handling of my payment request.

Cordially,

Benjamin Smith

Requesting investigation of a possible bank error

Amelia Robertson
11646 Flat Ridge Road
Rockytop, CO 64345

March 8, 2004

Reference: Amelia Robertson, Checking Account
010030337007

Julianna Williamson
Personal Banking Specialist
Colorado Federated Bank
22 Ski Slope Pass
Rockytop, CO 64345

Dear Julianna Williamson:

I believe I may have discovered an error in my February checking account statement. Could you please check into this and help me reconcile the discrepancy?

My statement shows a deposit February 26 of $280. The next day, February 27, a check for $872 was returned for non-sufficient funds, and I was assessed a $20 overdraft fee.

My records indicate, however, that the February 26 deposit was actually for $2,800, which would more than have covered the February 27 check.

Attached is a copy of my February 26 deposit receipt.

Please call me with your assessment of this situation. You may reach me weekdays at 787-1500.

Thank you for helping me resolve this situation as promptly as possible. I look forward to hearing from you within the next few days.

Sincerely,

Amelia Robertson

Deposit receipt attached

Even if you're certain the other person is in error, initially express your view with an open mind. You'll get better cooperation, and you could be wrong!

Step 1: Request specific information or action.

Step 2: Cover relevant background and details.

Although you may be tempted to express feelings about a check mistakenly returned for non-sufficient funds, stick to the facts.

Step 3: Provide contact information.

Step 4: Reiterate action and/ or thank.

Anticipate resistance? Use Template 2

Template 2 is most appropriate when you can anticipate resistance in response to your request. In these situations, you want a persuasive approach.

Disputing denial of a loan or credit card

Martin Langford
1 Rangeline Road
Rolling Ranch, TX 99989

November 26, 2004

Customer Service Representative
First America Bank
P.O. Box 1180
Wormington, DE 19899-1180

Dear Customer Service Representative:

Step 1: Request specific information or action.

Please reconsider my application for a First America Visa card. I believe my original "pre-approved" application has been denied in error.

Step 2: State reasoning and relevant information.

On October 1, I was denied a credit card based on "accounts with past due balances." As your letter suggested, I obtained a copy of my credit report, which lists every account I've ever held as "reported with no adverse information."

Step 3: State or restate details needed for compliance.

If this was, in fact, a legitimate offer to which I responded, I would appreciate your taking a second look at my credit history—or providing a legitimate reason for my denial. A copy of my original application is attached.

Step 4: Reiterate request, demonstrating confidence.

I look forward from hearing from you in the next few weeks with either good news or a reasonable explanation for my denial.

Thank you for your reconsideration,

Martin Langford

Attachment: original First America Visa card application

Disputing fee increase or new fee

Niles Proudlock
802 32nd Street
Motor City, MI 54545

September 20, 2004

Reference: Checking Account 231121448118

Beverly McFarland, President
Second National Bank
Second National Place
Motor City, MI 54545

Dear Beverly:

In a salutation using someone's first name only, either a comma or colon is appropriate.

Step 1: Request specific information or action.

I have noticed new ATM fees on my last two bank statements but don't recall receiving a notice explaining the reason for these fees. Could you please explain why I'm now being charged every time I use an automated teller machine? I do not feel I should be charged, especially without notice, for using ATMs.

Step 2: State reasoning and relevant information.

As you probably know, I've banked with you for nearly 20 years. In the last few years, I've found ATMs a convenient solution to my odd work schedule, which means often handling my banking before or after banking hours.

I've also appreciated the fact that I could use the most convenient ATM, even if it wasn't one at a Second National branch, all of which tend to be located on the outskirts of town. The fact that so many ATMs have been available to me, free of charge, is no doubt a key reason I've stayed with Second National in spite of my moving several times to different homes and different jobs around the city.

Step 3: State or restate details needed for compliance.

I do not feel I should be charged to use ATMs to conduct my banking business, and further feel that the fees, totaling $12.50, on my last two statements, those for July and August, should be refunded to me.

Step 4: Reiterate request, demonstrating confidence.

Please call or write me to fully explain your policies regarding ATM fees and how I might receive a refund of these fees charged without my consent. Phone: 321-5678.

Yours truly,

Niles Proudlock

Disputing a charge

Timothy Mayhern
911 Rolling Rock Ridge
Mountain Valley, MT 12123

June 23, 2004

Customer Service Representative
MasterCard Cardholder Services
Second National Bank
Farfield, VT 65655

Dear Customer Service Representative:

Please remove the May 9 Hospitality Hotel charge of $89 from my account; this charge was placed on my account in error.

I did reserve a room with Hospitality Hotel in Houston for this date and held the reservation with my MasterCard, but two days prior to this date I canceled the reservation. Because the hotel's policy allows for cancellations up until 6 p.m. the day of arrival, Miss Taylor at the hotel assured me I would not be charged.

I have also called the hotel, whose staff assures me the charge will be removed. However, because I am not completely confident the hotel will handle this competently, I decided to write to you as well.

I will look for an $89 adjustment on my next statement; if you have further questions about this situation or if you encounter difficulty meeting my request, please call me: 110/897-4643.

Thank you for removing this charge with your usual promptness. Unlike my dealings with Hospitality Hotel, my dealings with Cardholder Services have consistently been good ones. I appreciate that!

Yours truly,

Timothy Mayhern

Requesting a credit card limit increase

Step 1: Request specific information or action.

Step 2: State reasoning and relevant information.

Step 3: State or restate details needed for compliance.

Step 4: Reiterate request, demonstrating confidence.

Randal Scott
78 Everyman Lane
Middleton, Montana 36313

August 22, 2004

Visa Card Service Representative
Visa Card Services
500 Alabaster Way
Redmond, Rhode Island 54541

Dear Card Service Representative:

Please raise the limit on my Visa card account from its current $1,500 to $3,000.

As your records can confirm, I've kept this account in good standing for more than two years. I've never even been late with a payment and almost always pay above the minimum due each month. If you need more information about my financial situation, I would be happy to discuss this with you or complete any forms required to complete my request.

If I need do nothing more, please simply inform me of my new limit when it has been raised. If I need to provide more information, please write or call me with that information. My phone numbers are 990/555-8393 (daytime) or 990/555-9185 (evenings).

I would appreciate your prompt consideration of my request for this limit increase I feel completely confident I can handle.

Sincerely,

Randal Scott

Negotiating a payment schedule with a creditor

Joseph McQuinlain
906 West Orrington Avenue
Mission, NV 78978

Reference: Invoice Number 107056

July 23, 2004

Dr. Ethan Ransburg
Ransburg Orthodontics
8276 Park 100
Mission, NV 78978

Dear Dr. Ransburg:

Step 1: Request specific information or action.

I would like to propose establishing a regular payment schedule with you to help me pay my unpaid balance of $1,039.25.

Step 2: State reasoning and relevant information.

Because the recipient need do nothing to indicate compliance.

Unfortunately, my financial situation has changed rather significantly in the month since you removed Rebecca's braces. The company with whom I've worked for the past eight years recently laid me off, and I am in the process of finding another job.

Until my employment situation changes, I'd like to make monthly payments of $50. Enclosed is my first monthly payment.

Step 3 (State or restate details needed for compliance) is omitted.

As you can perhaps imagine, I find having to make these arrangements with you a little embarrassing. I fully expect this to be a temporary situation; you can expect full payment as soon as I've secured another job.

Step 4: Reiterate request, demonstrating confidence.

I hope you find this payment schedule acceptable. Thank you for your understanding in this matter.

Sincerely,

Joseph McQuinlain

If previous requests fail, try Template 3

Didn't get action from your Template 1 or Template 2 letter? A stronger letter may be warranted. Letters demanding action are most appropriate after two initial attempts, by phone or letter, have failed and a reasonable amount of time has passed.

Demanding action

When a follow-up letter is fruitless, you may opt to send a stronger letter. Use Template 3 to turn up the heat.

An attention line increases the likelihood someone will see your letter (even if the intended recipient has left the organization, for instance).

Step 1: State letter's purpose; acknowledge previous requests.

Step 2: Restate concern or request.

Step 3: State expectations and possibly next steps.

Step 4: State or restate details needed for compliance.

Step 5: Reiterate request and (optionally) thank.

Amelia Robertson
11646 Flat Ridge Road
Rockytop, CO 64345

April 6, 2004

Reference: Amelia Robertson, Checking Account 010030337007

Julianna Williamson
Personal Banking Specialist
Colorado Federated Bank
22 Ski Slope Pass
Rockytop, CO 64345

Attention: Arnold Albrecht, Branch Manager

Dear Julianna Williamson:

I'm concerned that I haven't seen a change in my account or heard from you regarding my March 8 letter. Will you help me, or should I be working with the branch manager?

My March 8 letter detailed how a $2,800 deposit was mistakenly entered as $280 and then resulted in a NSF check when the accurate balance should have covered the check. Attached is a copy of my first letter.

I expect my checking account to be corrected immediately and to be notified *within the next week to 10 days* that it has been corrected. If I do not hear from you in that time, I will discuss my concerns with your branch manager and lodge a formal complaint with the Colorado Department of Financial Institutions and the local Better Business Bureau.

My daytime phone number, again, is 787-1500.

I look forward to hearing from you with good news.

Sincerely,

Amelia Robertson
Attachment: March 8 letter

When to use Template 4

Use Template 4 to provide information that a company requests from you or to state action you are taking.

 Tip: You may be tempted to use Template 4 to voice a complaint. But if your key objective is getting an organization to right a wrong, Template 2 (persuading someone to take action) will be more effective.

Closing an account

If you've chosen to take definitive action, such as lodging a complaint with a third party or taking your business elsewhere, and you are not seeking a response from the original party, inform that individual or organization of your actions with a Template 4 letter. To gracefully end a long-standing business relationship, use Template 6 instead.

Step 1: Overview information or event letter will address.

Step 2: Provide information or describe event.

Step 3: Inviting recipient to contact you and providing contact information isn't appropriate if you do not expect—or want—follow-up contact.

Step 4: End with a lasting impression.

Martin Langford
1 Rangeline Road
Rolling Ranch, TX 99989

December 13, 1999

Customer Service Representative
First America Bank
P.O. Box 1180
Wormington, DE 19899-1180

Dear Customer Service Representative:

Please accept the enclosed check as payment in full on my First America Visa card, and close my account immediately.

The 5.9 percent interest rate for the first year was a great deal; however, both the mediocre service I've received during that year and the current, non-negotiable 14.9 percent interest rate make keeping the account foolish when so many better options are available.

Thanks, again, for a year of credit with an outstanding interest rate.

Sincerely,

Martin Langford

Check enclosed

To show appreciation, use Template 5

Template 5 is appropriate for acknowledging someone's act of kindness or display of outstanding service.

Recognizing good service

Timothy Mayhern
911 Rolling Rock Ridge
Mountain Valley, MT 12123

August 1, 2004

Jan Ericson, Customer Service Manager
MasterCard Cardholder Services
Second National Bank
Farfield, VT 65655

Dear Jan Ericson:

Step 1:
Acknowledge information or event.

Your representative, Oliver Randall, handled a disputed charge for me with such speed and professionalism that I felt compelled to write to you.

Step 2:
Elaborate as appropriate.

As the attached letter suggests, I was concerned that the merchant involved, Hospitality Hotel, would not act to remove the charge. When they did not do so even two weeks after they had agreed to, Mr. Randall took the initiative to call them directly and made sure the problem was resolved on the spot.

Step 3: End with a lasting impression.

Again, I commend Mr. Randall on his outstanding service; the quality of training your representatives receive is clearly evident in the above-and-beyond acts I've received many times from representatives at Second National Bank.

Thank you from a loyal customer!

Timothy Mayhern

Attachment

Tactfully take business elsewhere using Template 6

Most of us treat our relationships with companies more matter-of-factly than our relationships with individuals. If we decide to take our business elsewhere, for instance, we typically just say so (in a Template 4 letter) or just do it without saying so.

However, if you've had a long-standing relationship with a particular service provider, you may want to handle ending that relationship as a Template 6 letter. Template 6 "softens" bad news.

Closing a long-standing account

Step 1: Make general statement or restate request.

Step 2: Provide rationale behind negative response or bad news.

Step 3: State the negative response or bad news.

Step 4: An apology is not necessary here.

Step 5: End on a positive or encouraging note.

Niles Proudlock
802 32nd Street
Motor City, MI 54545

October 31, 2004

Reference: Checking Account 231121448118

Beverly McFarland, President
Second National Bank
Second National Place
Motor City, MI 54545

Dear Beverly:

Thank you for answering my questions about the ATM fees I've recently been seeing on my bank statements.

Thank you, too, for refunding your bank's fees from my previous two months' statements since I was not aware of your new fee policy. I also understand that what other banks charge Second National customers to use their machines is quite out of your control.

With the established fee structure of all the banks involved, though, I guess I should expect to pay extensive bank machine fees from now on. You see, I must use ATMs (to do my banking at odd hours), and Second National machines are rarely the most convenient for me.

Because I cannot accept such extensive fee increases, I will be moving my accounts to First Mutual, whose ATM fee policy seems much more reasonable.

Thank you for the nearly 20 years of outstanding service you've given my family. Especially when I've had concerns over the last few years about the bank's two buy-outs, you've been extremely helpful.

Yours truly,

Niles Proudlock

Letters for Medical and Insurance Concerns

Most letters in this area tend to be information-seeking or complaint-oriented. If your goal is to obtain information, use Template 1. But if your goal is to voice a complaint, your best approach is instead to persuade an insurance or healthcare provider to see things your way, use Template 2.

As always, keep such letters as brief and to-the-point as possible. But to help someone take the action you want, be sure to provide all important details, such as:

- Account or billing numbers.
- Insurance group or member numbers.
- Insurance claim addresses or phone numbers.
- Patient names.
- Birth dates (for identification purposes).
- Doctor names.
- Treatment or admission/release dates.
- Medication names.
- Dollar amounts.
- Person insured or financially liable (when not the patient).
- Guardian name and contact information (for minor patients).

Emotion generally has no place in such letters; keep your tone factual and business-like.

Medical and insurance letter samples

For straightforward requests, use Template 1

Requesting information or routine action from a healthcare provider or insurance company calls for a Template 1 letter. If your request is less-than-routine, and especially if you anticipate resistance, use Template 2 for a more persuasive approach.

Authorizing release of medical records

Step 1: Request specific information or action.

Step 2: Cover relevant background and details.

Step 3: Provide contact information.

Step 4: Reiterate action and/ or thank.

Angeline Rosario Smith
500 Crossroads Boulevard
Crossroads, IN 55554

May 22, 2004

Reference: Robert T. Smith, DOB 5/11/90

Dr. Leonard Eagleton
North Side Orthopedics
5902 Surgical Way
Crossroads, IN 55554

Dear Dr. Eagleton:

With this authorization, please release all medical records for my son, Robert T. Smith (birth date: 5/11/90), related to his knee injury last year.

Please send the records to:
> Dr. Theodore Murdock
> 9011 Medical Plaza
> Crossroads, IN 55554

If you need further information from me about my request, please call me at 555-0165.

Because we have an appointment for a second surgical opinion with Dr. Murdock on Friday, June 5, I'd appreciate your prompt attention to my request.

Sincerely,

Angeline Rosario Smith

Requesting medical information for an employer

David Valdez
401 Cactus Flower Lane
Scenic, Arizona 34362

May 6, 2004

Reference: David Valdez, DOB 7/3/45

Dr. Edith Worofski
6700 Shadeland Way
Scenic, Arizona 34362

Dear Dr. Worofski:

Step 1: Request specific information or action.

My employer has requested a letter from you detailing my medical condition. Could you please provide such a letter within the next week, if possible?

Step 2: Cover relevant background and details.

With my recent back injury, I have requested temporary placement in a position that does not require the bending and lifting I typically do in our warehouse. My employer is generally supportive but would like more information about what I should and should not do at work.

With this letter as authorization, please provide such information to:
    Mr. Sam Watson
    Mainline Pipe & Conduit
    10899 State Road 502
    Goodwell, Idaho 33333

Step 3: Provide contact information.

If you have questions about my request, please call me at work (909-5656) or home (909-5252).

Step 4: Reiterate action and/ or thank.

Thank you for you assistance.

Sincerely,

David Valdez

Requesting information on a pending claim

Sharon Epworth
6660 E. Chenille Court
Avondale, MI 65656

June 17, 2004

Reference: Insurance ID 306-58-5778

Claim Representative
Consolidated Healthcare
P.O. Box 3902
Hillside, NH 13121

Step 1: Request specific information or action.

Dear Claim Representative:

I need your assistance with a claim I filed more than six weeks ago but have yet to receive any information about.

Step 2: Cover relevant background and details.

Listing key details in table form can make responding to your letter easier.

Here are the relevant details:

Patient name and DOB:	Sharon Epworth, 6/28/57
Date of treatment:	April 28, 2004
Doctor's name:	Theodore Costello, DDS
Amount of claim:	$678.92

Step 3: Provide contact information.

Please call or write me with a response to my claim. You may reach me weekdays at 616/555-2262.

Step 4: Reiterate action and/ or thank.

I would appreciate your prompt attention to my claim.

Sincerely,

Sharon Epworth

Requesting a change in beneficiary

Isabelle Arlington
767 Carlington Court
Sansfield, ME 13631

March 1, 2004

Reference: Term Life Policy 3838740-83839

Policy Administrator
American Life Insurance Company
508 Insurance Way
Ravenswood, MD 41463

Step 1: Request specific information or action.

Dear Policy Administrator:

Effective immediately, please change the beneficiary on my term life insurance policy.

Step 2: Cover relevant background and details.

With my recent marriage, I'd like the following people named as beneficiaries on my policy:

Primary beneficiary: Simon Arlington
SSN 307-96-9878

Secondary beneficiaries: Charles and Mary Martinez
SSNs 322-85-9698 &
304-78-9646

Step 3: Provide contact information.

If you have questions about my request, please call me at 555/622-0393 (days) or 555/547-9630 (evenings).

Step 4: Reiterate action and/or thank.

Thank you for handling this important matter for me.

Sincerely,

Isabelle Arlington

Requesting information about a disease

Theresa Sausman
P.O. Box 6007
Grayson, Louisiana 22312

February 26, 2004

Leonard J. Robinson, Ph.D., Director
University of Louisiana Gerontology Center
901 North University Way
Research, Louisiana 22311

Dear Dr. Robinson:

Step 1: Request specific information or action.

Could you please send me information about Alzheimer's disease? My mother was recently diagnosed with this disease, and her doctor referred me to your organization for more information.

Step 2: Cover relevant background and details.

Here are my key concerns:
- What do we know about how quickly the disease typically progresses?
- What stages can we expect to go through?
- What medications seem most effective in postponing the onset of advanced symptoms?
- What, if anything, can we do to stimulate her mental functioning?

I would appreciate any literature or research results you can provide. I don't have a medical background, but (as you can imagine) I'm extremely interested in learning all I can to help my mother and our family to live with this difficult disease.

Step 3: Provide contact information.

If you need more information about my request, please call me at 696/455-9878.

Step 4: Reiterate action and/or thank.

Thank you for your assistance. This information will be invaluable to my family.

Sincerely,

Theresa Sausman

Disputing a straightforward billing error

Step 1: Request specific information or action.

Step 2: Cover relevant background and details.

Step 3: Provide contact information.

Step 4: Reiterate action and/ or thank.

Lisa Connerley
80706 Inlet South Drive
Seaside, FL 82565

August 12, 2004

Reference: Invoice 10227, Lisa Connerley, DOB 4/8/57

Office Manager
Rochelle Gunderson, M.D.
10178 South Shore Drive
Seaside, FL 82565

Dear Office Manager:

My August 4 statement of charges contains an error, and I'd appreciate your making an adjustment as soon as you can.

After I left your offices last Tuesday, I noticed that my statement lists a $68 charge for x-rays. While Dr. Gunderson and I discussed a possible x-ray, we ultimately decided it was not necessary and that my ankle was merely sprained. I'm sure Dr. Gunderson can verify that she did not order an x-ray.

For your convenience, a copy of my statement is attached. If you have any questions, please call me: 555-7825.

Thank you for addressing this promptly with my insurance company, United Heathcare, with whom you filed this claim.

Sincerely,

Lisa Connerley

Attachment: August 4 statement of charges

When persuasion may be needed, use Template 2

Template 2 is most appropriate when you can anticipate resistance in response to your request. In these situations, you want a persuasive approach.

Disputing a less-than-straightforward billing error

To add a personal touch, call for the office manager's name (and its spelling!), and address your letter to him or her.

Step 1: Request specific information or action.

Step 2: State reasoning and relevant information.

Step 3: State or restate details needed for compliance.

Step 4: Reiterate request, demonstrating confidence.

Kimberly Lynch
Rural Route 1040-B
Greenfield, NE 12625

May 18, 2004

Reference: Invoice 20187, Kimberly Lynch, DOB 3/11/60

June Steward, Office Manager
Pro Labs of America
12 Enterprise Way
Greenfield, NE 12625

Dear Ms. Steward:

I recently received a second notice for lab charges my insurance company tells me I am not responsible to pay. Please remove these charges from my account immediately, and stop sending me these insulting letters. (Copies of your letters and one from my insurance company are attached.)

As a preferred provider, your organization has agreed to provide services for "usual and customary rates." My insurance company, United Healthcare, has explained to me that I am not responsible for fees above the "usual and customary rates," to which you have agreed and for which United Healthcare has already paid you.

I hope this letter clears up the matter, but if I can provide more information, please call me at 555-8732.

I'm willing to assume that these letters have resulted from a misunderstanding and that your company will quickly resolve this situation—without sending me more form letters.

Thank you,

Kimberly Lynch

Attachments

Disputing denial on insurance coverage or a claim

Lionel Moore
11323 North Right Road
Persistence, PA 21215

October 14, 2004

Reference: Claim 70505022, Policy 10209-45849

Marcus Ellenberger, Claims Adjuster
ABC Healthcare Systems
4022 Insurance Way
Refusal, IA 91191

Dear Mr. Ellenberger:

Step 1: Request specific information or action.

Please reconsider your denial to pay for my daughter's Retin-A prescription. This is a medication that certainly should be—and in the past, has been—covered under our policy.

Step 2: State reasoning and relevant information.

My daughter's dermatologist, Dr. E.R. Whitney, has prescribed this medication for acne several times in the last two years. This is the first time we've had any difficulty receiving reimbursement. Enclosed is a copy of the doctor's Verification of Medical Need form, which she submitted to you last month.

Step 3: State or restate details needed for compliance.

Please reconsider this claim (I've also enclosed a copy of the claim), and if you will not reimburse us, please explain why. You may reach me days or evenings at 555/201-8111.

Step 4: Reiterate request, demonstrating confidence.

Thank you for your understanding in this matter. I look forward to hearing from you soon.

Sincerely,

Lionel Moore

Enclosures: Verification of Medical Need form
Copy of original claim

Arranging for monthly payments

Andrew Puckett
6809 Garden Court
Green Valley, VA 41641

January 20, 2004

Reference: Invoice 13567-562

Pamela Armstrong
Accounts Administrator
St. Mathews Hospital
2000 Hospital Way
Fenton, Massachusetts 69654

Dear Pamela Armstrong:

The fees on my January 12 statement seem to be in order. I would like to work with you to establish a regular payment schedule to help our family pay our unpaid balance.

As you might suspect, this automobile accident has hit my family hard financially. Even with medical insurance, the bills are much more than we can afford immediately.

I'd like to suggest monthly payments of $200. This amount is the very most we can afford especially in light of other expenses related to the accident. Enclosed is my first monthly payment.

I've never been comfortable owing large amounts of money to a creditor. Believe me, if I had any choice at all, you would already have payment in full.

I hope you find this payment schedule acceptable. Thank you for your understanding in this matter.

Sincerely,

Andrew Puckett

Complaining about medical services or staff

Sandra Sharpe
3096 East River Road
Greening, NY 20645

July 16, 2004

Reference: Patients Sandra Holson, DOB 5/4/65 and
James Sharpe, DOB 9/15/62
Date of service: June 5, 2004

Dr. Nelson Frye, Director
National MedCheck Centers
10 Market Place
Greening, NY 20645

Dear Dr. Frye:

Step 1: Request specific information or action.

Earlier this summer my husband (then my fiancé) and I received the most incompetent medical care from one of your doctors that either one of us has ever received. I would strongly encourage you to remove him from your medical staff.

Step 2: State reasoning and relevant information.

Just days before our wedding, we both developed a mysterious rash from head to toe. It seemed serious enough to warrant a visit to your East Side MedCheck early on a Friday evening, June 5. (The wedding was that Sunday.)

Because the recipient need do nothing to indicate compliance, **Step 3** (State or restate details needed for compliance) is omitted.

Dr. Henry Simpleton saw us and quickly diagnosed it as scabies, which I was appalled to learn results from a parasite laying eggs under the skin! I was almost more appalled by his prescription: an insecticide with which we were to dowse ourselves from head to toe morning and night for several days. The diagnosis seemed odd, but we dutifully followed his advice, yes, even on our wedding day and night.

Imagine my amazement when a friend (not a doctor) asked us, just as we were leaving the next day for our honeymoon, where we had gotten into so much *poison ivy!* (We had even told Dr. Simpleton we'd both been working in the yard all that Friday!)

Step 4: Reiterate request, demonstrating confidence.

I will never return to a National MedCheck Center. I sincerely hope this doctor is not representative of your entire staff, and I encourage you to get rid of such incompetence before a more serious mistake costs someone much more than a romantic wedding night.

Sincerely,

Sandra Sharpe

Template 3 letters that demand action may alienate doctors, office managers, or insurance company representatives with whom you plan to retain a relationship. If previous attempts fail to yield results, your best option may be to appeal to a third party, for instance, a state insurance regulatory board, the AMA, or your Congressional representative. For such letters, use Template 4.

When to use Template 4

Use Template 4 to provide information when persuasion isn't needed.

Terminating poor medical care

Step 1: Overview information or event letter will address.

Step 2: Provide information or describe event.

Step 3: Invite recipient to contact you and provide contact information.

Step 4: End with a lasting impression.

Tina Louise Littrell
60 Canyon Trail
Pueblo, NM 64524

April 27, 2004

Reference: Tina Louise Littrell, DOB 7/8/76

Dr. Angelique Rhude
7283 Medvale Pike, Suite 200
Pueblo, NM 64524

Dear Dr. Rhude:

I will no longer be returning to your office for my gynecological care. Please forward my medical records to:

Dr. Sylvia Lopez
7287 Medvale Pike, Suite 302
Pueblo, NM 64524

I'm a relatively new patient, and I've found working with your office dehumanizing. Your staff is neither courteous nor conscientious. When I call for lab results, I'm put on hold for long periods without explanation; I end up explaining the same information to several people, each of whom expresses the same ignorance and indifference about my questions. Then I'm told "The doctor will call you back." Yet I never get a return call.

I have also yet to schedule an appointment for which I didn't have to wait at least 45 minutes. Couldn't appointments be scheduled better to show respect for your patients' time?

If you would like to hear more about one patient's first impressions, I would be happy to discuss my experiences further. You can call me during work hours at 315-6457.

I'm sure your reputation as a physician is well-deserved, but I would never feel comfortable entrusting my care to a doctor whose office management shows so little respect for her patients.

Sincerely,

Tina Louise Littrell

🏷️ **Tip:** To gracefully end a long-standing relationship with a healthcare provider, use Template 6 instead. When the relationship is or was important to you, a Template 6 letter can "soften" the bad news.

Use Template 5 to say, "Thanks!"

To acknowledge outstanding service you've received from a healthcare or insurance professional, use Template 5.

Showing appreciation for good care or service

Step 1: Acknowledge information or event.

Step 2: Elaborate as appropriate.

Step 3: End with a lasting impression.

Lara Gilman-Thomas
1470 Chantilly Way, Apartment 3B
Lakeside, MI 54648

January 22, 2004

Donté Green, M.D.
2089 Professional Way
Lakeside, MI 54648

Dear Dr. Green:

Your care of my father during his recent heart difficulties was nothing less than exceptional, and I'd like to thank you.

I imagine thousands of doctors are, like you, quite competent with the technical aspects of performing an angioplasty. But I've rarely (if ever) seen a doctor handle the less technical aspects with such grace. You met with my father several times, always with diagrams in hand, to make sure he understood and was comfortable with what was happening to him. You answered all of our questions with patience and genuine concern, never confounding us with medical language—as I've so often experienced with doctors.

My profession is that of an adult educator, so I know quite a bit about how adults learn, how fearful they can be when they feel ignorant, and how they like to be treated as they learn. Your skills in this area are among some of the best I've seen among *my* professional colleagues. I commend you and thank you.

Respectfully,

Lara Gilman-Thomas

Soften bad news with Template 6

If you've had a long-standing relationship with a particular healthcare provider, you may want to handle ending that relationship as a Template 6 letter. Template 6 "softens" bad news.

Terminating a long-standing healthcare relationship

Step 1: Make general statement or restate request.

Step 2: Provide rationale behind negative response or bad news.

Step 3: State the negative response or bad news.

Step 4: An apology is not necessary here.

Step 5: End on a positive or encouraging note.

Tina Louise Littrell
60 Canyon Trail
Pueblo, NM 64524

April 27, 2004

Reference: Tina Louise Littrell, DOB 7/8/76

Roscoe Pierce, M.D., and staff
11290 West Austin Drive
Pueblo, NM 64524

Dear Dr. Pierce and staff:

Thank you for your care and attention during the last six years I've been a patient. You've always been competent and attentive with my medical needs and have worked hard to accommodate, even on short notice, any appointment changes my challenging work schedule has required me to make.

As you may already be aware, your move to the far west side of town, creating a 30-minute drive for me each way, has made keeping my appointments even more challenging.

Because I cannot expect this situation to become easier for either of us, I feel I must find a physician more centrally located. I'd like next Thursday to be my last appointment with you.

I regret having to make this decision. I have always trusted your judgment regarding my care, and I would greatly appreciate your recommendation of a physician with offices on the north side of town. Could we discuss this when I see you on Thursday?

Kind regards,

Tina Louise Littrell

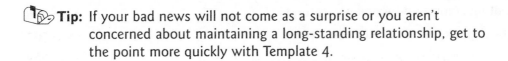 **Tip:** If your bad news will not come as a surprise or you aren't concerned about maintaining a long-standing relationship, get to the point more quickly with Template 4.

Letters to
Government Agencies

When dealing with big government agencies, such as the Internal Revenue Service, Social Security Administration, or Department of Veterans Affairs, clear, detailed, concisely-written letters may be the only way to get the action you need.

Government agency letter samples

For information requests, use Template 1

If your goal is to request general information about government programs, regulations, taxes, and the like, use Template 1.

To ensure that you get the information you need, use a reference line to list pertinent identification or policy numbers. Then state your request as early in the letter as possible and make sure you're specific about exactly what you need.

Requesting a copy of military records

Step 1: Request specific information or action.

Step 2: Cover relevant background and details.

Step 3: Provide contact information.

Step 4: Reiterate action and/ or thank.

Captain Dean L. Harris, USA
5006 North Rangeford Avenue
Mountain Springs, UT 54645

February 2, 2004

Reference: Service/Social Security Number 308-57-2333

Personnel Records Officer
National Personnel Records Center
9700 Page Boulevard
St. Louis, MO 63132-5100

Dear Personnel Records Officer:

Please send me a copy of my discharge papers from the U.S. Army.

I lost track of my own copy in a move several years ago but now need it to apply for disability benefits. I served from September 1982 to December 1997 and was honorably discharged with the rank of captain.

If you have questions about my request, please call me at 801/987-6543.

Thank you for your assistance and quick response.

Sincerely,

Captain Dean L. Harris, USA

Requesting a form for a VA loan

Corporal Peter Yancy, USMC
210 Apple Tree Court
Green Groves, VA 12345

June 25, 2004

Reference: Service/Social Security Number 365-85-5002

Veterans Affairs Officer
Department of Veterans Affairs
819 Vermont Avenue NW
Washington, DC 20420

Dear Veterans Affairs Officer:

Step 1: Request specific information or action.

Please send me a copy of VA form 26-1880, Request for Determination of Eligibility and Available Loan Guaranty Entitlement.

Step 2: Cover relevant background and details.

I have never applied for a VA home loan before but understand I'm entitled to do so as a veteran of the U.S. Marines who has served more than 181 days. I served from June 1977 to February 1979 and was honorably discharged with the rank of corporal.

Step 3: Provide contact information.

If you have questions about my request, please call me at 555/654-1245.

Step 4: Reiterate action and/or thank.

I would appreciate your immediate response to my request.

Sincerely,

Corporal Peter Yancy, USMC

Reporting a lost or stolen Social Security card

Step 1: Request specific information or action.

Step 2: Cover relevant background and details.

Step 3: Provide contact information.

Step 4: Reiterate action and/ or thank.

Connie Chen
9975 Redwood Row
Pacific, CA 44321

August 17, 2004

Reference: Social Security Number 375-50-6010

Social Security Administration
6401 Security Boulevard
Baltimore, MD 21235

Dear Social Security Representative:

Could you please send me guidelines and any forms I would need to apply for a duplicate Social Security card?

I'm not sure what happened to my original card; I believe it's been lost for some time.

If you have questions about my request or if this is a process I can handle by telephone, please call me at 555/123-4567.

Thank you for your prompt attention to my request for a new card.

Sincerely,

Connie Chen

Claiming Social Security benefits

Step 1: Request specific information or action.

Step 2: Cover relevant background and details.

Step 3: Provide contact information.

Step 4: Reiterate action and/ or thank.

Chase Crawford
211 South Palm
White Wave, FL 13930

January 13, 2004

Reference: Social Security Number 311-69-9767

Social Security Administration
6401 Security Boulevard
Baltimore, MD 21235

Dear Social Security Representative:

Please send me the paperwork necessary to claim Social Security benefits.

My wife, Marleen J. Tuney, died recently, and I understand that my minor children and I are now eligible to claim benefits.

Please call me at 555/321-7548 if I can provide additional information about this request.

I would greatly appreciate your timely response.

Sincerely,

Chase Crawford

Reporting change of address to the Social Security Administration

Step 1: Request specific information or action.

Step 2: Cover relevant background and details.

Step 3: Provide contact information.

Step 4: Reiterate action and/ or thank.

Jerold Dryfuss
6767 Red Oak Road
Traders' Pass, MI 33490

November 4, 2004

Reference: Social Security Number 304-88-6588

Social Security Administration
6401 Security Boulevard
Baltimore, MD 21235

Dear Social Security Representative:

Effective immediately, please begin sending my Social Security benefits checks to my new mailing address.

My previous address:

Jerold Dryfuss
298 Green Tree Lane
Traders' Pass, MI 33490

My new address:

Jerold Dryfuss
6767 Red Oak Road
Traders' Pass, MI 33490

If I need to complete a form to accomplish this request, please send or fax me a copy of that form. Please note that my telephone number, too, has changed. My new (telephone and fax) number is 555/231-4575.

I would appreciate your help in preventing any delay because of my change of address.

Sincerely,

Jerold Dryfuss

Requesting statement of Social Security earnings/Medicare benefits

Jacob Alev
700 Mapleleaf Ridge
Heartland, OH 67577

July 2, 2004

Reference: Social Security Number 322-56-5665

Social Security Administration
6401 Security Boulevard
Baltimore, MD 21235

Dear Social Security Representative:

Step 1: Request specific information or action.

Please send me a copy of the Request for Earnings and Benefit Estimate Statement form.

Step 2: Cover relevant background and details.

I will be retiring within the year and need to determine the approximate benefits I will be eligible for at that time.

Step 3: Provide contact information.

If faxing me a copy of this form is more convenient, please do so. My phone and fax number is 555/741-9874.

Step 4: Reiterate action and/or thank.

Thank you for your assistance in getting me this form.

Sincerely,

Jacob Alev

Claiming military life insurance benefits

Step 1: Request specific information or action.

Step 2: Cover relevant background and details.

Step 3: Provide contact information.

Step 4: Reiterate action and/or thank.

Barbara Emerson
1010 Canyon Ridge Road
Cliffside, AZ 11223

May 24, 2004

Reference: Service/Social Security Number 345-78-1245
National Service Life Policy Number 01887978797889

Veterans Affairs Officer
Department of Veterans Affairs
819 Vermont Avenue NW
Washington, DC 20420

Dear Veterans Affairs Officer:

As the beneficiary of my husband's National Service Life Insurance policy, I am requesting payment of this policy's settlement.

My husband, Andrew L. Emerson, U.S. Air Force colonel, retired, died April 1, 2004, in Cliffside, Arizona. A certified copy of the death certificate is enclosed. My husband served from October 1956 to November 1970 and received an honorable discharge.

My phone number, in case you need more information, is 555/457-3698.

Thank you for your prompt assistance in disbursing our life insurance benefits.

Sincerely,

Barbara Emerson

enclosure

Requesting a copy of a birth certificate or other document from a county clerk's office

Leda Springfield
35 Lava Pass
Volcano, Hawaii 12564

January 18, 2004

Reference: Tasha Elaina Springfield, D.O.B. January 5, 1984

Records Clerk
County Clerk's Office
67 Kaimu Grove
Volcano, Hawaii 12564

Step 1: Request specific information or action.

Dear Records Clerk:

Please send me a copy of my daughter's birth certificate. We wish to apply for a Social Security card for her, but we have been unable to locate her birth certificate to do so.

Step 2: Cover relevant background and details.

Her name:	Tasha Elaina Springfield
Date of Birth:	January 5, 1991
Place of Birth:	Mercy Hospital, Oahu, Hawaii
Parents' Names:	James T. and Leda R. Springfield

Step 3: Provide contact information.

A check for the $3 processing fee is enclosed. In case you have questions about this request, my phone number is 555/784-9685.

Step 4: Reiterate action and/ or thank.

Thank you for your prompt assistance in providing a duplicate birth certificate.

Sincerely,

Leda Springfield

Requesting travel information from a state tourist information bureau

Step 1: Request specific information or action.

Step 2: Cover relevant background and details.

Step 3: Provide contact information.

Step 4: Reiterate action and/or thank.

Rebecca Hochman
5077 North Elm Street
Bakersfield, OH 45655

February 18, 2004

Tourists' Bureau Representative
Michigan Tourists' Bureau
1234 Tourist Drive
Great Lakes, MI 54321

Dear Tourists' Bureau Representative:

I understand that your office provides a tourist information packet for travel in northern Michigan; I'd like to receive this packet as soon as possible.

My family and I plan to camp in northern Michigan this summer for the first time. We could use any information you can provide on state parks, camping facilities both inside and outside the state parks, camping fees, and (of course) outdoor activities and noteworthy sites in northern Michigan.

I understand that this information packet is free; if I am mistaken or if you offer additional resources for which you charge a fee, please call. Our phone number is 555/987-1237.

Thanks for your assistance. We're looking forward to seeing your beautiful state.

Sincerely,

Rebecca Hochman

Requesting information or forms for renewing a passport

Darrel Carter
90088 Magnolia Lane
Dancing, LA 47444

February 18, 2004

Reference: Passport Number 032954252

Step 1: Request specific information or action.

National Passport Center
Federal Building
Chicago, IL 60604

Dear Passport Center Representative:

Please send me guidelines and/or forms for renewing my passport.

Step 2: Cover relevant background and details.

I will be traveling outside the U.S. in approximately three months.

Step 3: Provide contact information.

If you need additional information to complete my request, please call me at 555/123-9874.

Step 4: Reiterate action and/ or thank.

Thank you for your prompt assistance.

Sincerely,

Darrel Carter

For less-than-routine requests, use Template 2

Requests that are unusual, beyond routine, or likely to run into resistance call for a Template 2 approach. The best approach to complaining is to, instead, request action.

Disputing denial of VA benefits

Deborah Klein
22202 Spiny Tail Row
Cactus, NM 23445

March 27, 2004

Reference: Service/Social Security Number 306-56-3112

Veterans Affairs Officer
Department of Veterans Affairs
819 Vermont Avenue NW
Washington, DC 20420

Dear Veterans Affairs Officer:

Step 1: Request specific information or action.

Please review the enclosed claim; I believe it was denied in error.

Step 2: State reasoning and relevant information.

The form letter I received did not explain why this claim was denied; the claim is, however, well within the guidelines of this standard benefit to which military veterans are entitled.

Step 3: State or restate details needed for compliance.

To summarize the details:

Nature of claim:	Reimbursement for military burial marker
Standard benefit:	"Average cost" for purchase of marker
Amount of claim:	$732
Diseased:	Edward J. Tudrow
Branch/Service dates:	U.S. Marines, October 1974 to March 1990
Discharge:	Honorable

Copies of my original claim, receipt for purchase of the marker, death certificate, and letter of denial are enclosed.

Step 4: Reiterate request, demonstrating confidence.

Thank you for your cooperation in looking into this matter. I hope to receive either reimbursement or a letter fully explaining the reason for denial.

Thank you,

Deborah Klein

Enclosures

Disputing denial of Medicare benefits

Step 1: Request specific information or action.

Step 2: State reasoning and relevant information.

Step 3: State or restate details needed for compliance.

Step 4: Reiterate request, demonstrating confidence.

Franklin McKenny
9404 Lone Star Road
Long View, TX 45667

December 7, 2004

Reference: Medicare case number 68868

Social Security Administration
6401 Security Boulevard
Baltimore, MD 21235

Dear Social Security Representative:

My mother was recently denied coverage on a claim for continued physical therapy due to a hip injury. We believe the treatment should be covered and ask you to reverse your denial of coverage.

Without continued physical therapy, quite frankly, my mother would not be able to walk; in place of the nominal cost of regular physical therapy, we would no doubt be looking at the cost of a wheelchair and its accompanying costs. A letter of medical necessity from her doctor is attached to this letter, along with a copy of the claim.

If I can provide additional details to assist you in rendering a decision, please call me at 555/546-5647.

Thank you,

Franklin McKenny

Enclosures

Disputing amount of Social Security check

Step 1: Request specific information or action.

Step 2: State reasoning and relevant information.

In this case, **Step 3** (State or restate details needed for compliance) was covered in Step 2.

Step 4: Reiterate request, demonstrating confidence.

Glenda O'Shea
123 Muenster Court
Cheddar, WI 67981

May 11, 2004

Reference: Service/Social Security Number 311-65-6487

Social Security Administration
6401 Security Boulevard
Baltimore, MD 21235

Dear Social Security Representative:

I am writing to request a recomputation of the amount of my Social Security checks.

Last March, I received a letter from you stating that my monthly checks would be for $632.48. A copy of this letter is enclosed, along with a copy of my check stub. As you can see, my check for $448.32 is $184.16 less than what I was told I would receive.

Because I now rely on these checks, I would greatly appreciate a prompt resolution to this situation and an adjustment as soon as possible.

Thank you,

Glenda O'Shea

Enclosures

Disputing amount of income tax refund

Lee Chung
23 Tulip Tree Court
Farmgrove, IN 74877

September 18, 2004

Reference: SSN 312-54-7965

IRS Representative
Internal Revenue Service
600 S. Maestri Place
New Orleans, LA 70130

Dear IRS Representative:

Step 1: Request specific information or action.

Please review my 2003 income tax return for what I believe to be a simple bookkeeping error, and issue an adjustment check as soon as possible.

Step 2: State reasoning and relevant information.

The refund check I received for $135.68 should actually have been for $1,356.80 according to my records. Because I received no letter explaining the discrepancy, I'm assuming it was, in fact, merely a bookkeeping error.

Step 3: State or restate details needed for compliance.

To summarize:

Refund due	$1,356.80	
Refund paid	135.68	
Balance due	$1,221.12	(plus any interest accrued to date)

Copies of your original refund check and letter are enclosed. If I can provide further details, please call me at 555/657-8956.

Step 4: Reiterate request, demonstrating confidence.

Thank you for looking into this matter promptly and sending me the remainder of my refund.

Thank you,

Lee Chung

Enclosures

Disputing amount of income taxes owed

Nelam Patel
11 North Willow Lane
Swan Lake, NC 83892

September 7, 2004

Reference: Social Security numbers 366-75-9224
and 306-76-8551

IRS Representative
Internal Revenue Service
915 2nd Avenue
Seattle, WA 98174

Dear IRS Representative:

Step 1: Request specific information or action.

My husband and I received a letter stating that we owe $3,050 on our 2003 taxes. I believe we do not owe anything for 2003 and also believe I know the reason for the discrepancy. Please review our tax return, and make the proper adjustment.

Step 2: State reasoning and relevant information.

The exact amount of $3,050 is what I paid quarterly in my '03 estimated tax payments. (My husband's employer withheld his '03 taxes.) I feel certain that one of these estimated tax payments has not been taken into account.

Step 3: State or restate details needed for compliance.

Here is a summary of the dates and amounts of my '03 estimated tax payments. (Copies of the canceled checks and payment vouchers are attached.)

Quarter	Amount of check	Date of check
1st	$ 3,050.00	3/15/03
2nd	3,050.00	6/16/03
3rd	3,050.00	9/15/03
4th	3,050.00	1/15/04

I also noticed that my third quarter check included only my Social Security number, not both numbers as they traditionally do. Could this be the "lost" check? If I can provide more information, please call me at 555/877-6123.

Step 4: Reiterate request, demonstrating confidence.

Thank you for looking into this matter and making any necessary adjustments as soon as possible.

Thank you,

Nelam Patel

Enclosures

Disputing property tax assessment

Uri Asomof
660 East Chestnut Way
Modock, RI 39390

April 2, 2004

Reference: Property Tax Assessment for 660 East Chestnut Way

Hendricks County Assessor
1 Government Plaza
Modock, RI 39390

Dear Tax Assessor:

Step 1: Request specific information or action.

I believe an error has been made in the assessment of my property; I would appreciate your looking into this matter as quickly as possible and sending me a revised assessment.

Step 2: State reasoning and relevant information.

The taxes I paid in 2002 on this property were $1,256.89. With no major improvements to the property in 2003, how could the assessment have been raised to $1,760.98 (a 40-percent increase)?

I'm also aware that my neighbors to the north and south, each with properties and homes similar in value, paid 2003 assessments of $1,315 and $1,278, respectively.

Step 3: State or restate details needed for compliance.

Please explain your justification for this $504.09 increase or provide a revised assessment as soon as possible.

Step 4: Reiterate request, demonstrating confidence.

Thank you for your prompt attention in clearing up this obvious mistake.

Thank you,

Uri Asomof

 Tip: Template 3, used for letters demanding action, is probably not likely to get action with a government agency if your Template 1 or Template 2 letter fails. You'll probably just alienate a government employee without the authority to take action on your behalf anyway.

When to use Template 4

Use Template 4 to provide information when a persuasive approach isn't needed.

Reporting a name change due to marriage or divorce to the Social Security Administration

Step 1: Overview information or event letter will address.

Step 2: Provide information or describe event.

Step 3: Invite recipient to contact you and provide contact information.

Step 4: End with a lasting impression.

Gerianne Raines
50 Poplar Grove
Beetussle, TN 93930

October 19, 2004

Reference: Social Security Number 304-65-6575

Social Security Administration
6401 Security Boulevard
Baltimore, MD 21235

Dear Social Security Administration Representative:

Please change my Social Security records to reflect my name change due to marriage.

Maiden name: Gerianne Grace Mitchell
Married name: Gerianne Mitchell Raines

Enclosed are copies of my marriage certificate and my current (outdated) Social Security card.

If you need other information to complete my request, please call me during work hours at 777/854-3614, or send me the necessary form and directions.

Thank you for your assistance in bringing my records up to date.

Sincerely,

Gerianne Raines

Notifying the Social Security Administration of a spouse's death

Step 1: Overview information or event letter will address.

Step 2: Provide information or describe event.

Step 3: Invite recipient to contact you and provide contact information.

Step 4: End with a lasting impression.

Rosa Allende
8808 North Aspen
Rocky Top, CO 34733

May 2, 2004

Reference: Social Security Number 312-82-7772

Social Security Administration
6401 Security Boulevard
Baltimore, MD 21235

Dear Social Security Administration Representative:

I am writing to inform you of my husband's death and to determine whether I am now eligible for survivor's benefits.

My husband, John J. Allende, died February 10. A copy of his death certificate is enclosed. At the time of his death, he was receiving monthly checks for $589.56.

Please send me information as to my eligibility as well as any necessary forms I need to complete.

I appreciate any assistance you can give me in this matter.

Sincerely,

Rosa Allende

Responding to an IRS audit notice

Step 1: Overview information or event letter will address.

Step 2: Provide information or describe event.

Step 3: Invite recipient to contact you and provide contact information.

Step 4: End with a lasting impression.

George E. Grant
34 Keeler Way
St. Paul, MN 55101

May 2, 2004

Reference: Social Security Number 312-82-7772

Internal Revenue Service
316 N. Robert Street
St. Paul, MN 55101

Dear IRS Representative:

Enclosed are copies of the documents you requested for your audit of my 2003 tax return.

My full name:　　George Eliot Grant
SSN:　　　　　　302-82-4565

Documents enclosed:
- Business expense record for my home-based business.
- Mileage log for business use of automobile.
- Documentation for charitable deductions.

If I can provide other information, please write, or call me at home: 555/684-8589.

I'll be happy to provide any information I can to help answer your questions.

Sincerely,

George E. Grant

Letters and E-mails to U.S., State, or Local Government Officials

Sometimes writing to your elected officials is the best, or perhaps the only, way to get action you need. If the issue is a popular or volatile one, you can assume that those government officials involved will be inundated with letters.

Concisely written letters that get to the point, specify the action you want taken, and include all necessary, *relevant* information will more likely stand out.

An important note: All government officials and politicians have e-mail addresses these days; simply visit the Website of the appropriate government agency or the politician's home page.

Congress and local official letter samples

For straightforward requests, use Template 1

If your goal is to request general information from an elected representative, use Template 1.

State your request as early in the letter as possible and make sure you're specific about exactly what you need.

Requesting an elected official's position on an issue

Randall Lawrence
Old Hickory Row
Big Sky, Texas 78233

April 3, 2004

The Honorable Harold Carter
P.O. Box 12068
Capitol Station
Austin, Texas 78711

Dear Senator Carter:

Step 1: Request specific information or action.

What is your position on penalties for juvenile offenders of "adult" crimes such as murder?

Step 2: Cover relevant background and details.

As a father of two elementary-school-age children, I've been particularly troubled by the apparent increased incidence of pre-adolescents committing horrendous, even premeditated crimes, often on school grounds. What's particularly troubling is a juvenile penal system that allows a convicted criminal under age 18 to go free when he or she turns 18!

I understand that a bill proposing dramatic changes in the juvenile penal code could reach the Senate floor later this term. What is your position on this issue so vital to our children's safety both now and in the future? What is the bill precisely, and how do you plan to vote?

Step 3: Provide contact information.

If you have questions about my request or would like to speak with me, please call me at 555/362-5656 (daytime) or 555/362-5891 (evenings).

Step 4: Reiterate action and/ or thank.

I look forward to hearing your position on this issue. Thank you for your service to our community.

Sincerely,

Randall Lawrence

To be persuasive, use Template 2

Requests that are other-than-routine and situations calling for a persuasive approach call for Template 2.

Requesting enhancement of city services

Renata Berkowitz
1256 E. 52nd Street
Beaverton, Vermont 00600

March 6, 2004

The Honorable Abigail Riley
Mayor of Beaverton
City-County Building, Room 100
1011 North Pennsylvania
Beaverton, Vermont 00600

Dear Mayor Riley:

Step 1: Request specific information or action.

How does one go about getting a much-needed sidewalk on several blocks that, for safety reasons, need one now more than ever before?

Step 2: State reasoning and relevant information.

The blocks I'm referring to are the 1200 and 1300 blocks of East 54th Street (between Carrollton and Carvel Avenues). The absence of sidewalk on either side of the street has been a problem for years, but with the opening of the Monon walking trail nearby, 54th Street has become a major pedestrian thoroughfare.

Throughout the day and especially on weekends, hundreds of walkers, joggers, skaters, and bikers—of all ages—make their way to the trail via 54th Street. When they get to these blocks, they have no choice but to trample on someone's grass or walk in the very busy street! Aren't services such as sidewalks the reson we pay property taxes?

Step 3: State or restate details needed for compliance.

I've already written to the Department of Public Works, who suggested I write to you. I would appreciate your response— as well as information on other specific steps I can take to make this sidewalk a reality. If calling is more convenient, my phone numbers are 555/659-3585 (days) and 555/154-5647 (evenings).

Step 4: Reiterate request, demonstrating confidence.

Thank you for your prompt response to my request. I feel certain that the safety concerns my request involves make it a top priority for the city's use of our tax dollars.

Thank you!

Renata Berkowitz

Encouraging political support on an issue

Riccardo Manendez
667 Beechtree Boulevard
Grainfields, Kansas 15858

June 20, 2004

The Honorable Barbara M. Arsdale
Kansas State House of Representatives
State Capitol Building
Topeka, Kansas 66612

Dear Senator Arsdale:

Step 1: Request specific information or action.

I oppose the phone company's plan to implement measured-service pricing, and I'd appreciate your support on this issue.

Step 2: State reasoning and relevant information.

In spite of the phone company's claims that measured-service pricing would not increase the average person's phone bill, my friends in other states in which measured-service pricing was allowed would beg to differ. In Missouri and Nebraska, measured-service pricing has resulted in a 10- to 20-percent price increase for the people with whom I've spoken.

Step 3: State or restate details needed for compliance.

Basic telephone service should continue to be made available to all Kansas citizens, even those who can barely afford the service at its current price. Next to food, clothing, and shelter, telephone service today is almost a necessity of life—not to mention a life-saver in countless situations.

Step 4: Reiterate request, demonstrating confidence.

I hope you support me in my view of measured-service pricing and will vote to prevent its implementation.

Sincerely,

Riccardo Manendez

Opposing an elected official on an issue

Mr. Harvey Greenwald
1000 Great Plains Way
Blizzard, North Dakota 32624

January 18, 2004

The Honorable Harold F. Scott
Mayor of Blizzard
300 Market Street
Blizzard, North Dakota 32624

Dear Mr. Mayor:

I oppose the renovations you propose to make to our great historic landmark, the Boswell Theatre. Please reconsider your position on this issue.

Your strategy to increase the seating capacity of the theater so that it may draw larger crowds and bring more world-class theatrical performances to the city may be financially sound. But everything I've heard and read in recent weeks leads me to believe such a renovation would destroy the theater's architecture, some of the best of its kind in this country.

Can't we find financially viable uses for this local and national treasure that do not require its destruction? Other possibilities have been raised; which of these have been seriously considered? Must we always sacrifice the beauty and history of our city for short-sighted financial gain?

I would appreciate a response to my letter if for no other purpose than to more fully explain your position. I trust, however, that the outcry your renovation plan has raised will give you pause to consider a solution that both I and a majority of your constituency can support.

Sincerely,

Mr. Harvey Greenwald

Step 1: Request specific information or action.

Step 2: State reasoning and relevant information.

To make your argument more persuasive, express understanding of your reader's perspective; then reinforce your own.

Step 3: State or restate details needed for compliance.

Step 4: Reiterate request, demonstrating confidence.

 Tip: Template 3, used for letters demanding action, is probably not likely to get action with an elected official. A better approach might be to subtly suggest, in a Template 2 letter, that you and others are likely to withdraw your support if the elected official does not represent your views (as he or she was elected to do) while in office.

When to use Template 4

Use Template 4 to provide information when a persuasive approach isn't needed.

Announcing withdrawal of your support for an elected official

Step 1: Overview information or event letter will address.

Step 2: Provide information or describe event.

Step 3: Inviting recipient to contact you and providing contact information isn't appropriate if you do not expect—or want—follow-up contact.

Step 4: End with a lasting impression.

Mr. Harvey Greenwald
1000 Great Plains Way
Blizzard, North Dakota 32624

October 18, 2004

The Honorable Harold F. Scott
Mayor of Blizzard
300 Market Street
Blizzard, North Dakota 32624

Dear Mr. Mayor:

I regret to inform you, Mr. Mayor, that I will not be voting for you in the November election.

Your massive destruction of treasured city landmarks and green spaces over the past four years demonstrates a resource management policy I was not aware of when I voted for you. I can no longer lend you my support.

The economic growth of our city must take place with respect, not disdain, for its historic and environmental resources.

While I can appreciate the economic growth Blizzard has experienced in the past few years, I'm afraid it has come at a cost I, for one, can no longer tolerate.

Sincerely,

Mr. Harvey Greenwald

To show your support, use Template 5

When your elected official takes an action you approve of or appreciate, tell him or her with a Template 5 letter!

Supporting an elected official's position on an issue

Step 1:
Acknowledge information or event.

Step 2:
Elaborate as appropriate.

Step 3: End with a lasting impression.

Rosa Allende
8808 North Aspen
Rocky Top, Colorado 34733

February 2, 2004

The Honorable Darlene Emerson-Sanchez
House of Representatives
1711 Longworth House Office Building
Washington DC 20515

Dear Representative Emerson-Sanchez:

The stance you've taken on mandating the National Do-Not-Call Registry is admirable, and I extend to you my support.

More than 50 million Americans registered their phone numbers on the National Do-Not-Call list that the Federal Trade Commission (FTC) instituted to ban commercial telemarketing companies from calling them. I was among these Americans. This issue received tremendous media attention, especially after that federal judge from Oklahoma City blocked the list from going into effect, claiming that the FTC did not have the authority to keep the registry. Within a day, you and your fellow congressional representatives passed a bill giving the FTC authority to mandate the Do-Not-Call list. Telemarketers have been invading our homes long enough. We are all tired of having precious private family time interrupted by phone calls from companies looking to make a quick sale. Hanging up repeatedly and other strategies for dealing with these calls have proved futile.

Thank you for your consistent, hard-line position. Despite the fact that this action continues to be challenged, millions of Americans like me will continue to support representatives like you, who consistently stand up for what is right.

Respectfully,

Rosa Allende

Expressing appreciation for service to the community

Step 1:
Acknowledge information or event.

Step 2:
Elaborate as appropriate.

Step 3: End with a lasting impression.

Jamey O'Riley
5040 Moore Way
Beaverton, Vermont 00600

August 21, 2004

The Honorable Joanna Aaronson
Vermont State Senate
115 State Street
Montpelier, Vermont 05602

Dear Representative Aaronson:

Thank you for your diehard support for development of the Monon walking trail, formerly the old north-south rail line, running through Beaverton.

This beautiful, paved trail has completely transformed our city. People of all ages, races, shapes, and sizes now come together to use the trail to bike, skate, run, walk, and generally enjoy the beauty of the North Side. I understand that the trail will eventually run all the way downtown. What a wonderful way to continue to connect our communities and offer a safer venue for all these forms of outside recreation.

I'm generally not terribly well-informed on local politics and issues; however, I've been so thrilled with the addition of the trail to our city that I made a point to find out who was responsible for its development simply so I could thank her.

Thank you!

Jamey O'Riley

To tactfully deliver bad news, use Template 6

To acknowledge your long-standing support for an elected official even when you must withdraw your support, use Template 6.

 Tip: If your bad news will not come as a big surprise or you aren't compelled to honor a long-standing relationship, get to the point more quickly with Template 4 instead.

Withdrawing support for an elected official

Randall Lawrence
Old Hickory Row
Big Sky, Texas 78233

October 18, 2004

The Honorable Harold Carter
The State Senate
100 Capitol Station
Austin, Texas 78711

Step 1: Make general statement or restate request.

Dear Senator Carter:

Your interest in our state's juvenile penal code has led me to write to you before on this issue.

Step 2: Provide rationale behind negative response or bad news.

Your public statements and voting record clearly indicate that you believe our current juvenile detention system needs no changes—or if it does, the changes are too costly to pursue.

In your position statement, you acknowledge that our prison system should rehabilitate rather than condemn youngsters; I agree. Yet I've seen no evidence that our juvenile detention centers serve as anything more than a holding tank until these youngsters reach 18. Then, of course, by law, they're released.

Step 3: State the negative response or bad news.

Step 4: An apology is not necessary here.

I do not believe you will adequately represent my views in our Senate or will support change in the juvenile detention system. Because I feel this change is critical to the safety of our communities, I will not be voting for you in the upcoming election.

Thank you for taking the time to hear one (formerly loyal) constituent's concerns.

Step 5: End on a positive or encouraging note.

Sincerely,

Randall Lawrence

Letters About Real Estate and Legal Concerns

In a situation that involves a real estate transaction or a legal issue—closing the sale on a new home, for example, or settling a lawsuit—the task of writing important letters usually falls to an attorney, an agent, or some other professional hired to represent you. But that doesn't mean there won't be times when you'll benefit from knowing how to craft persuasive letters with "legal-ease"—the subtle but powerful writing style used by the professionals. For example, maybe you need to write to someone about a small claims complaint you filed without a lawyer. Or you may find yourself needing to know how to write a letter asking an attorney to represent you. Or perhaps you want to bid on a property for sale without the services of a real estate agent.

For basic cases like these, you'll find the guidelines we provided in the section on consumer letters helpful. You can follow that section's tips on making a good first impression with your letter, using the right tone, selecting the right person to whom to send your letter, keeping your letter the right length, and setting a deadline for a response.

Even so, there are some additional pointers that relate specifically to real estate and the world of law that can help you write the best letter possible, even when you're not a legal professional, a mortgage broker, a real estate agent, or anyone else who knows the legal implications of what you do, and do not, put in writing. This section gives you tools to help you write careful, ethical letters about the most basic legal and real estate matters—letters that can get your point across without entangling you in the age-old fear of "saying the wrong thing." You'll also find sample letters that, like the other samples in this book, can be adapted to your own unique situation. As usual, our samples are accompanied by step-by-step instructions.

Please note that we caution you not to write e-mails about sensitive legal matters or real estate transactions; mailed letters are often more appropriate for reasons we discussed in Chapter 2. Also note that we do not include samples of legally binding documents such as agreements, wills, affidavits, or power-of-attorney forms.

The sample letters included in this section are simply that—*letters*. As with any other letter, you address these letters to a particular recipient and your signature is just a way of closing your letter and saying goodbye! For help with composing legal documents, contracts, or anything that needs a signature to be legally binding, always consult a legal or real estate service.

Also, because we do not have professional experience in the legal arena or real estate market, this book is not a substitute for legal counsel. Always use your best judgment and rely on advice from a professional before sending any letter that deals with legal or real estate issues.

Real estate and legal letter samples

For straightforward requests, use Template 1

Remember that requests for information or routine action call for a Template 1 letter. Again, if you anticipate any disagreement by your recipient, Template 2 (persuading others to take action) would be more appropriate.

Requesting information about a home

To ensure that you get the information you need, make sure you're specific about exactly what that is.

Francesca Martin
16 Tangerine Lane
Mystic, Connecticut 06355

March 22, 2004

Marlene Hague
77 Greenbriar Way
Temecula, California 92592

Dear Ms. Hague:

Step 1: Request specific information or action.

I am interested in learning more about your property for sale. Please send me the following information:
- The year the property was built and the life of the foundation.
- The specifications of your heating and cooling system—gas, electric, oil, and so on, with any applicable warranty information.
- The floor plan.
- Records regarding any current or past infestation by termites or other pests.
- Existing or proposed construction or development in the region.
- Government restrictions, requirements, limitations, or classifications of the property, including flood and other zoning classifications.
- The number of closets and/or pantries in the home.

Step 2: Cover relevant background and details.

In addition, I would like photographs of the front and back exterior of the house, the bathroom, and the kitchen.

Step 3: Provide contact information.

I am looking for a home south of the Los Angeles area and plan to make a purchase within a year based on the information I receive. You can call me at 990/555-1009.

Step 4: Reiterate action and/or thank.

Thank you for your assistance, and I look forward to receiving this information.

Sincerely,

Francesca Martin

Tip: Make a response more likely by enclosing a stamped, addressed envelope as a courtesy to the recipient.

Requesting a home inspection report

Step 1: Request specific information or action.

Step 2: Cover relevant background and details.

Step 3: Provide contact information.

Step 4: Reiterate action and/ or thank.

Candy Summerlein
799 Trinket Cove
Maplehill, Louisiana 54245
980/555-3039

March 27, 2004

John L. McAloney
Home Inspection Engineer
Quality Home Inspection Services
203 Bell Drive North
Maplehill, Louisiana 54245

Dear Mr. McAloney:

Could you please provide me with a detailed report of the home inspection you performed at 23 West Bend Way on March 22?

My husband and I, who intend to purchase the property at this location, would like to review the report, as our real estate broker had a hospital emergency and has been unable to discuss the details of the report with us.

Please send this information before April 9. My address and phone number appear above. I appreciate your prompt response.

Sincerely,

Candy Summerlein

Requesting information for legal purposes: court records

Kelly Barth
11 Poca Path
Oxford, Ohio 45056
513/555-0889

May 31, 2004

Joanie Russell
Clerk
Hamilton County Probate Court
William Howard Taft Center
230 East Ninth Street
Cincinnati, OH 45202

Dear Ms. Russell:

Step 1: Request specific information or action.

I am writing to request three certified photocopies of the determination of heirs held in the case *Barth* vs. *Montgomery Savings & Loan*, case number 2456X.

Step 2: Cover relevant background and details.

I have enclosed a check in the amount of $3.00 to cover the fee for these records and a stamped, self-addressed envelope, as instructed on your Website.

I am selling the property I inherited from my aunt, Marjorie Clark. The buyer's agent has requested documentation held in the aforementioned case.

Step 3: Provide contact information.

Step 4: Reiterate action and/ or thank.

If you have any questions, please call me at (814) 555-5555. Please send me the records by June 14, 2004. I appreciate your prompt response.

Sincerely,

Kelly Barth

Requesting information for legal purposes: credit history

Kelly Barth
11 Poca Path
Oxford, Ohio 45056
513/555-0889

May 15, 2004

James Morgan
Credit Manager
Expedia Credit Reports
3i Big Bell Road
Breezewood, Pennsylvania 15533

Dear Mr. Morgan:

Step 1: Request specific information or action.

I authorize you to release information about my credit history to Cindy Malone, Mortgage Loan Officer, at the following address.

> Hamilton Savings Bank
> 205 Pequot Drive
> West Milford, New Jersey 07480

Step 2: Cover relevant background and details.

I recently applied for a mortgage loan with Ms. Malone. She requested information concerning my credit history. I authorize the investigation of my credit information for the purpose of this loan application.

Your release of my credit information is authorized whether the information is of record or not. I do hereby release you and all persons, agencies, agents, employees, firms, companies, or parties affiliated with you from any damages resulting from providing such information.

Step 3: Provide contact information.

Step 4: Reiterate action and/ or thank.

If you have any questions, please call me at (814) 555-5555. Please send Ms. Malone this information before June 7. I appreciate your prompt response.

Sincerely,

Kelly Barth

Requesting information for legal purposes: medical records

Corey Joseph
11 Augustine Place
Silver Springs, Maryland 20910

August 29, 2004

Anita Quirija
Acute Physical Therapy Services
202 Broad Street
Columbia, Maryland 21044

Dear Ms. Quirija:

Step 1: Request specific information or action.

I authorize you to release to the law firm of Houser & Southern any and all records of medical treatment I received during May 2002 through June 2003. Please release all records, including those detailing initial consultation, history, examination, tests, diagnosis, notes, summaries, laboratory reports, test reports, x-rays, CAT scans, EKGs, EEGs, treatment, and prognosis.

Step 2: Cover relevant background and details.

Please send these records to

Ronald Riccardo, Esq.
Houser & Southern
99 Windy Trail
Joppa, Maryland 21085
(555) 555-1111

Mr. Riccardo represents the defendant against which I have filed a complaint of negligence for the injuries I sustained in a slip-and-fall accident.

Step 3: Provide contact information.

For the purposes of locating my records, my Social Security number is 307-96-9878 and my date of birth is May 21, 1971.

Step 4: Reiterate action and/ or thank.

If any fee is payable for these records, please call me at (555) 555-5555 before processing this request. Thank you for your prompt attention to this matter.

Sincerely,

Corey Joseph

Requesting the services of a lawyer

Corey Joseph
11 Augustine Place
Silver Springs, Maryland 20910
(555) 555-5555

September 30, 2004

Brandon Egidio, Esq.
Graham, Groome, and Egidio
39 Van Esten Street
Columbia, Maryland 21044

Dear Mr. Egidio, Esq.:

Step 1: Request specific information or action.

Could you please provide me with attorney representation in the liability lawsuit I have filed against Anderson Associates, the management company for the apartment complex where I live?

Step 2: Cover relevant background and details.

On February 16, 2000, I slipped on a patch of ice and fell on rocky pavement, dislocating my shoulder, breaking a tooth, and straining my neck. An EMG showed that I suffered nerve damage as a result of the accident. I filed a complaint with the county court, *pro se*. Attached are all records of my medical treatment, records of lost wages due to absence from work, and a detailed report of my incident. I continue to receive medical treatment for the injuries I received and find that it is too difficult to continue to manage my case on my own. I would like to schedule a meeting with you to discuss my case and your fees for service.

Step 3: Provide contact information.

Step 4: Reiterate action and/or thank.

Please write or call me before October 28. I appreciate your prompt response.

Sincerely,

Corey Joseph

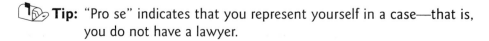 **Tip:** "Pro se" indicates that you represent yourself in a case—that is, you do not have a lawyer.

Making an offer on a home

Step 1: Request specific information or action.

Step 2: Cover relevant background and details.

Step 3: Provide contact information.

Step 4: Reiterate action and/ or thank.

Francesca Martin
16 Tangerine Lane
Mystic, Connecticut 06355

August 22, 2004

Marlene Hague
77 Greenbriar Way
Temecula, California 92592

Dear Ms. Hague:

Please consider my offer of $210,000 for your beautiful two-bedroom home at 77 Greenbriar Way in Temecula, California, Lot 23 in NorthcoastCounty, seller's deed #1243. Please contact me at 990/555-1009 as soon as you can to tell me whether you accept my offer, and send me a purchase and sale contract at your earliest convenience.

I have attached a deposit of $1,000 to secure my bid on your property. Also attached is a letter from Country Savings stating that it has preapproved me for a 30-year mortgage loan for an home costing up to $260,000, with a 10 percent downpayment and an interest rate of 6.25 percent.

My mortgage company informs me that I would be able to close on this home purchase within six weeks of the execution of our purchase and sale agreement. Please note that my offer is contingent upon adequate financing, an independently conducted property assessment, a home inspection, and the accuracy of the features of the property as represented by the seller (see attached list). This offer expires on January 1, 2005.

Thank you for considering this offer.

Sincerely,

Francesca Martin

Terminating the services of a real estate buyer's agent

Francesca Martin
16 Tangerine Lane
Mystic, Connecticut 06355

October 5, 2004

Genora Coltrain
Mickey B. Connor Real Estate Agency
3 Garden Road
Mystic, CT 06355

Dear Ms. Coltrain:

Step 1: Request specific information or action.

Whereas, on September 1, 2003, I, Francesca Martin, entered into an agreement with you, Genora Coltrain, to retain your services as a buyer's agent, an agreement that under the law is subject to a right of rescission by me, and I have determined to exercise this right, I hereby notify you that I rescind that agreement under the laws in the State of Connecticut. I have decided to look for property in another state and no longer require your services to help me find a property to purchase in Connecticut.

Step 2: Cover relevant background and details.

Step 3: Provide contact information.

This right of rescission was sent via certified mail on October 5, 2004, at 11:02 a.m.

Please call me at 990/555-1009 if you have any questions. Thank you for your services.

Step 4: Reiterate action and/ or thank.

Sincerely,

Francesca Martin

Changing a beneficiary designation

Step 1:
Request
specific
information or
action.

Step 2:
Cover relevant
background
and details.

Step 3:
Provide contact
information.

Step 4: Reiter-
ate action and/
or thank.

William Donnelly
80 Pinecone Street
Oklahoma City, Oklahoma 92750

November 22, 2004

Hal Brook
Policy Assistant
Colonial Green Investment Firm
19 Castle Drive
Manchester, New Hampshire 12791

Re: Account Number F09-245-9
William Donnelly
Benficiary Change

Dear Mr. Brook:

I wish to change the beneficiary on the above-referenced account. Presently the policy provides for the following individual as beneficiary:
Marilyn Donnelly

As of the fifth day of December 2004, the beneficiary should be changed from the aforementioned listed individual to the following:
William Donnelly, Jr.
Social Security number 322-85-9698

Should there be additional documents that need to be completed in order to effect this change, please mail those documents to me at my address above. If you have any questions, please contact me.

Thank you,

William Donnelly
555/555-3701

Community Action and Fund-Raising Letters

Working with volunteers and asking for financial contributions to good causes can be especially challenging. When the cause is worthwhile, however, these letters are well worth a try.

Tact, of course, is critical in these types of letters. Always remember that your letter's recipients give of their time or money *voluntarily*. Their giving is always a choice, and that choice deserves respect. Therefore, you won't find Template 3 letters, letters demanding action, in this section.

While the saying may be true that "if you want something done, ask a busy person," never forget that the reader of your letter will undoubtedly be that busy person. So get to the point, say it in few words, specify exactly what you want done, and include all necessary, *relevant* information.

Community action and fund-raising letter samples

For straightforward requests, use Template 1

Requesting information or routine action from someone calls for a Template 1 letter. If your request is less-than-routine and especially if you anticipate resistance, use Template 2 for a more persuasive approach.

Requesting information

Step 1: Request specific information or action.

Step 2: Cover relevant background and details.

Step 3: Provide contact information.

Step 4: Reiterate action and/ or thank.

Robin Darnell
9482 Sunnyside Avenue
Makepeace, Indiana 45678

May 22, 2004

The Reverend Terrance Manley
United Church Federation
610 East 16th Avenue
Makepeace, Indiana 45678

Dear Reverend Manley:

I'm writing to you for information on getting involved with the United Church Federation's antiviolence activities.

Your organization is becoming quite well-known for its nondenominational approach to bringing the power of prayer to sites of violent crime. I would very much like to be a part of such an effort.

Could you please tell me how I might become a participant in your Immediate Action Prayer Chain? I can be reached at 123-6758.

Thank you for your leadership of such powerful action against violence in our community. I look forward to hearing from you so that I may join you in your work.

Sincerely,

Robin Darnell

An alternative to complaining: Requesting information

Instead of writing an emotion-filled letter complaining about a potentially volatile situation, which could possibly alienate the letter's recipient, start by objectively requesting information using Template 1.

Step 1: Request specific information or action.

Step 2: Cover relevant background and details.

Step 3: Provide contact information.

Step 4: Reiterate action and/ or thank.

William Alderson
466 Forest View Road
Hampton, Alabama 88907

May 30, 2004

Mr. Lawrence Hamilton, President
Hamilton-Jones Commercial Properties, Inc.
80 Blacktop Drive
Hampton, Alabama 88907

Dear Mr. Hamilton:

As a long-time resident of the Near North Hampton neighborhood, I hope you can answer a few questions about the shopping mall your company plans to begin building here in the next few months. Could you tell me please:

- On what date do you expect construction to begin?
- Under what city and county permit numbers will you be operating?
- On what date(s) did public hearings occur regarding the rezoning of this property from residential to commercial use?

The families in this area will be greatly affected by your proposed construction. I would very much appreciate your cooperation in providing this information, either by mail or phone (205/555-6556).

Thank you,

William Alderson

This approach is more likely to get results than an angry complaint letter that begins: "The last thing we need in this neighborhood is another shopping mall! I demand to know under what authority you can change zoning laws to build your malls wherever you like, no matter who it affects...."

When persuasion may be needed, use Template 2

Template 2 is most appropriate when you can anticipate resistance in response to your request. In these situations, you want a persuasive approach.

Soliciting participation in an activity

Step 1: Request specific information or action.

Step 2: State reasoning and relevant information.

Step 3: State or restate details needed for compliance.

Step 4: Reiterate request, demonstrating confidence.

Arland Weaver
606 Pinetree Pass
Mountain Valley, Wyoming 45466

June 5, 2004

Cynthia Thomas
511 Pinetree Court
Mountain Valley, Wyoming 45466

Dear Cynthia:

Please consider taking an active part in bettering our environment by participating in a new neighborhood curbside recycling program.

Recycling your steel and aluminum cans, plastic bottles and milk jugs, and newspapers is easy and goes a long way to protecting our environment. Recycling reduces landfill waste, air pollution caused by incinerator fumes, and even poor ground water quality.

If you're willing to give curbside recycling a try, you need do nothing. Within the next week you will receive a storage tub and complete guidelines on how the program works. Our neighborhood association will cover your cost for the first six months of service. After that (should you decide to continue with the program), the cost is minimal: typically $3 to $5 per month.

If you prefer not to participate in the program, please call our neighborhood association office (555-2312), and someone will gladly pick up your storage tub.

Thanks for considering curbside recycling. We on the recycling committee feel certain you'll find it one of the easiest ways you can help us all to protect our environment.

Thank you,

Arland Weaver

Persuading someone to accept a leadership position

Step 1: Request specific information or action.

Step 2: State reasoning and relevant information.

Linda Ridgefield
1578 Sycamore Grove Lane
Brookfield, New York 20131

May 29, 2004

Shelly Rudolph
1585 Sycamore Grove Lane
Brookfield, New York 20131

Dear Shelly,

Would you consider heading up a Crime Watch effort on our block?

Several neighbors including Joan Kern, Tim Allison, John Merrick, and I thought you would be perfect in this role; and we'd be thrilled to help by hosting meetings, providing refreshments, or doing whatever needs to be done.

You would be our neighborhood's primary contact with our Police Department representative, Officer Ralph St. John. In a brief conversation I had with him, Officer St. John told me that getting a Crime Watch group going doesn't take much effort: planning quarterly meetings, leading those meetings, and keeping neighbors in touch with one another seems to be the gist of it.

We thought you would be perfect for the role because everyone knows you, you're a devoted neighbor to so many of us, and your home office keeps you around the neighborhood a little more often than the rest of us.

Step 3: State or restate details needed for compliance.

Step 4: Reiterate request, demonstrating confidence.

Would you be willing to consider taking on this role? I'll call you next week—after you've had some time to think about it—to find out what you're thinking, and you're also welcome to call Officer St. John directly for more information about what would be involved. He's at the 48th Precinct, phone 549-5454.

We've all talked about the need for this in the past; we all agree it's important. Will you help us make it a reality?

We'd all owe you one!

Linda Ridgefield

Soliciting contributions

Marvin Armstrong
4303 Grand Spires Way
Grand City, UT 67867

March 27, 2004

Jenny Stevenson
4327 Grand Spires Way
Grand City, UT 67867

Dear Jenny Stevenson:

Step 1: Request specific information or action.

Would you consider making a donation this year to the American Heart Association?

Step 2: State reasoning and relevant information.

Heart disease is the number one killer of both men and women. Yet recent advances in research, including balloon angioplasty, enhanced transplant methods, and less invasive surgical procedures have helped thousands to prolong their lives; increased awareness of blood cholesterol levels and the importance of exercise have helped millions to prevent future heart problems.

How do these changes happen? In part, through our donations to the American Heart Association. As your neighbor, I encourage you to consider a donation this year.

Step 3: State or restate details needed for compliance.

To make a donation, simply fill out the enclosed pledge card and include it, with your check, in the envelope provided. (Don't forget a stamp!) Your donation is, of course, tax deductible.

Step 4: Reiterate request, demonstrating confidence.

On behalf of the American Heart Association, I thank you for considering a contribution this year. Please mail your contribution by April 24, 2004.

Sincerely,

Your neighbor, Marvin Armstrong

enclosures

Confirming others' participation in an activity

The purpose of this type of letter is to continue to persuade volunteers to participate, so Template 2 is most appropriate.

Letters addressed to individuals, rather than to "Soup Kitchen Volunteers," for instance, will get a better response.

Step 1: Request specific information or action.

Step 2: State reasoning and relevant information.

Step 3: State or restate details needed for compliance.

Step 4: Reiterate request, demonstrating confidence.

Mary Beth Alsopp
Soup Kitchen Chair
First Central Church
201 North Central Avenue
Southern Cross, Mississippi 64648

March 1, 2004

Olivia Cox
5564 Acre Lane
Southern Cross, Mississippi 64648

Dear Olivia:

The time has come to get our new soup kitchen off the ground! If you're receiving this letter, you've expressed an interest in the past in helping out with this important community outreach project. Well, it's time!

Just how you can get involved, and how much time you give, is completely up to you. Here are a few possibilities:

- Help prepare food (two-hour shifts).
- Help serve food (two-hour shifts).
- Help to pick up supplies or food (one- to three-hour shifts).
- Help in set-up or clean-up (one- and two-hour shifts).
- Help in promoting the kitchen (time varies by activity).

The kitchen is scheduled to serve its first weekly meal on May 3. Please call or sign up at the church to volunteer your time beginning Monday, March 29. (Church office phone is 655-8287.) Many activities need to happen prior to May 1, so the sooner you can volunteer with something, the better our opening should be!

Thank you, again, for expressing interest in helping to get our new kitchen rolling!

In gratitude,

Mary Beth Alsopp
Soup Kitchen Chair

 Tip: Template 3, used for letters demanding action, is probably one sure method to alienate potential volunteers and contributors. A better approach might be to *tactfully remind* someone of action he or she agreed to take but hasn't, in a Template 2 letter.

When to use Template 4

Use Template 4 to provide information when a persuasive approach isn't needed.

Agreeing to participate in an activity

Because this letter is a response to another one, a first-name salutation is an appropriate option.

Step 1: Overview information or event letter will address.

Step 2: Provide information or describe event.

Step 3: Invite recipient to contact you and provide contact information.

Step 4: End with a lasting impression.

Samuel Bernstein
3004 East Ash Court
Middletown, Indiana 74947

June 4, 2004

Beth Ann Johnson
7971 Hollyoke Row
Middletown, Indiana 74947

Dear Samuel,

I received your notice about the East Creek cleanup on June 27, and I'd be happy to participate. I do have a few questions I'd like to ask, however.

- I have an 8 a.m. commitment to work out with a friend. Could I join the group shortly after 9 a.m.?
- Where is the cleanup starting, and where should I try to find you?
- Should I bring garbage bags, shovels, and so on, or do you expect to have plenty?

Could you give me a quick call with this information sometime before the cleanup? I'd appreciate it. My home number is 555-6574. (Leave a message during the day if you'd like.)

I'll see you at the cleanup!

Sincerely,

Samuel Bernstein

 Tip: To acknowledge receiving outstanding service, use Template 5.

Accepting a leadership position

When using a first name in the salutation, either a comma or a colon is appropriate ending punctuation.

Step 1: Overview information or event letter will address.

Step 2: Provide information or describe event.

Step 3: Invite recipient to contact you and provide contact information.

Step 4: End with a lasting impression.

Shelly Rudolph
1585 Sycamore Grove Lane
Brookfield, NY 20131

April 3, 2004

Linda Ridgefield
1578 Sycamore Grove Lane
Brookfield, NY 20131

Dear Linda,

As you probably suspected, I would be happy to head up a Crime Watch group. In fact, I think it might be a lot of fun— provided, of course, that I can count on you, Joan, Tim, and John for help.

Let's schedule a first meeting sometime in early June. That would give me the chance to talk to our police representative and sort out what needs to be done.

If you're serious about this, let's you and I go together to meet Officer St. John; that way, you can help me sort out the details. Then I'd be happy to take it from there. Please do call me later this week so we can discuss possible meeting times.

Crime Watch is something we've needed to get organized for a long time. I'll be happy to head up the effort—but remember, you're with me all the way, right?

Sincerely,

Shelly Rudolph

Refusing a request to serve or contribute

Step 1: Overview information or event letter will address.

Step 2: Provide information or describe event.

Step 3: Inviting recipient to contact you and providing contact information isn't appropriate if a return call isn't warranted.

Step 4: End with a lasting impression.

Olivia Cox
5564 Acre Lane
Southern Cross, Mississippi 64648

March 10, 2004

Mary Beth Alsopp
Soup Kitchen Chair
First Central Church
201 North Central Avenue
Southern Cross, Mississippi 64648

Dear Mary Beth:

I'm afraid I won't be able to help out with the soup kitchen as I had hoped.

Since I first expressed interest in helping out with the kitchen, my time has become significantly more limited. In January, I decided to return to school part-time; getting back into a routine of studying, attending classes at night, and continuing to work full-time is proving more difficult than I had expected.

If my schedule lightens up at all, I promise to call you. I really would like to help out with a cause I believe can make a real difference to the community. Best of luck in getting the soup kitchen off the ground!

Yours truly,

Olivia Cox

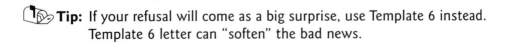 **Tip:** If your refusal will come as a big surprise, use Template 6 instead. Template 6 letter can "soften" the bad news.

To show appreciation, use Template 5

Template 5 is best for acknowledging someone's extra effort or generosity in service to a community.

Thanking others for their contributions or time

Letters addressed to individuals, rather than to "Crime Watch Volunteers," for instance, will come across as more sincere.

Step 1: Acknowledge information or event.

Don't stop with a generic thank you. Describe what this individual did so your recognition comes across as more sincere.

Step 2: Elaborate as appropriate.

Step 3: End with a lasting impression.

Shelly Rudolph
1585 Sycamore Grove Lane
Brookfield, New York 20131

June 12, 2004

Linda Ridgefield
1578 Sycamore Grove Lane
Brookfield, New York 20131

Dear Linda:

Well, our first meeting was a hit! I can't believe how many people showed up, and we have you to thank for such a great turnout.

Your idea to deliver "personal invitation" postcards was brilliant. Thanks for all the work you did to design a card, print cards up, and deliver them.

The real benefit to getting all our neighbors to show up, of course, is the ability we have now to spread the work around! I plan to make some calls later this month to make sure we don't lose our momentum, so let me know what role you'd like to take from here, okay?

Thanks, again, for helping to get things off to such a great start!

Sincerely,

Shelly

Acknowledging a refusal to serve or contribute

Acknowledging someone's refusal is not only common courtesy, it builds good-will and may lead to his or her future involvement.

Step 1:
Acknowledge information or event.

Step 2:
Elaborate as appropriate.

Step 3: End with a lasting impression.

Mary Beth Alsopp
Soup Kitchen Chair
First Central Church
201 North Central Avenue
Southern Cross, Mississippi 64648

March 18, 2004

Olivia Cox
5564 Acre Lane
Southern Cross, Mississippi 64648

Dear Olivia:

Thanks for your note explaining your inability right now to help out with the soup kitchen.

I wish you could be involved, of course, but I do understand, and I sincerely appreciate your letting me know so I can better plan for the volunteers we need.

You're always welcome, of course, to become more involved. We'll continue to need volunteers well into the future, so please let me know if your schedule allows you to participate.

Sincerely,

Mary Beth

To tactfully say no, use Template 6

If you you're dealing with a long-standing relationship you want to maintain, you may want to decline participation with a Template 6 letter. Template 6 "softens" bad news. However, if your refusal will not come as a big surprise or you haven't established a long-standing relationship, get to the point more quickly with Template 4 instead.

Refusing a leadership role

Robin Darnell
9482 Sunnyside Avenue
Makepeace, Indiana 45678

November 2, 2004

The Reverend Terrance Manley
United Church Federation
610 East 16th Avenue
Makepeace, Indiana 45678

Dear Reverend Manley:

Step 1: Make general statement or restate request.

Thank you for having the confidence in me to suggest that I lead a North Side recruitment effort for the United Church Federation's antiviolence activities. As you know from my regular involvement in the United Church Federation's work, your mission is one I firmly believe in and would like to support in any way I can.

Step 2: Provide rationale behind negative response or bad news.

I worry, however, that orchestrating a recruitment effort will take my time and effort away from the prayer work itself. To be completely honest with both you and myself, I'm drawn more to the work and also feel I would not be particularly good at heading up such an effort.

Step 3: State the negative response or bad news.

So while I'll be happy to participate in the recruitment effort if I can, I do not feel I should head it up.

Step 4: An apology is not necessary here.

Thanks for your understanding of my decision. I do have someone else in mind who I feel would be both willing and better-suited to lead the recruitment effort. I'll call you within the week to share my thoughts with you.

Step 5: End on a positive or encouraging note.

Warmest regards,

Robin Darnell

Resigning a leadership role

Step 1: Make general statement or restate request.

Step 2: Provide rationale behind negative response or bad news.

Step 3: State the negative response or bad news.

Step 4: An apology is not necessary here.

Step 5: End on a positive or encouraging note.

Shelly Rudolph
1585 Sycamore Grove Lane
Brookfield, New York 20131

December 15, 2004

Dear 1500-Block Neighbors:

Thanks, everyone, for your willingness to make our block a little safer with Crime Watch.

My role as coordinator over the last six months has been exhausting but completely rewarding. Thank you for helping me to get such an important effort rolling for our block.

With the birth of my second child just three months away, I feel the time has come for me to pass the role of coordinator along to someone else. A newborn and a toddler are all I feel I'll be able to manage by March, and I'm afraid Crime Watch might receive short shrift if I continue as coordinator.

So effective January 31, I'll be resigning as your Crime Watch coordinator.

Please, if you're willing to discuss taking on this role after January 31, or would simply like more information about what it involves, please call me (654-8214) before our January meeting.

So many people have devoted just as much time as I have in getting Crime Watch going on our block that I feel certain we can keep the momentum going. If you're moved to consider taking on the coordinator role, please do. I can assure you you'll get all the help you need to be successful.

Sincerely yours,

Shelly Rudolph

Letters and E-mails to
the Media

The different forms of media available to us can be extremely helpful in getting the word out about something we care about, from selling a used car to voicing an opinion on an issue to announcing a daughter's engagement.

Too few people take full advantage of this easy and inexpensive means of communicating to many people at once. The media exist, we should remember, to serve our interests as a civilized society. Your well-written letter or e-mail—a message that quickly gets to the point, delivers your message clearly and concisely, and includes all the information someone might need to respond—can prove a powerful vehicle for expressing yourself in public.

Media letter samples

For straightforward requests, use Template 1

Requesting information or routine action from someone associated with a newspaper, magazine, radio, or television station or program calls for a Template 1 letter. If your request is less-than-routine, and especially if you anticipate resistance, use Template 2 for a more persuasive approach.

Requesting information on placing a classified ad

Step 1: Request specific information or action.

Step 2: Cover relevant background and details.

Step 3: Provide contact information.

Step 4: Reiterate action and/or thank.

Katschuichi Yamamoto
700 Birch Road
Greentown, Illinois 60606

July 31, 2004

Classified Ad Representative
The Marion County Gazette
One Newspaper Row
Greentown, Illinois 60606

Dear Classified Ad Representative:

Please help me to place a classified ad in *The Gazette* for Sunday, August 9.

I've never advertised in *The Gazette* before, so I'm not sure how to go about it. But I've reviewed other ads in the paper, and here's what I'd like my ad to say:

Moving Sale August 15–16, 8 a.m. to 4 p.m.
8092 Trestle Way Court, one block east of 80th and Boulevard. Dining and bedroom furniture, small appliances, lawn equipment. Must sell; moving out of country.

Please call or write me to confirm my request and inform me of the cost of the ad and your payment policy. My home phone number is 845/254-9647.

I look forward to hearing from you and appreciate your assistance.

Sincerely,

Katschuichi Yamamoto

When persuasion may be needed, use Template 2

Use Template 2 when you anticipate resistance in response to your request.

Requesting a correction or retraction

Step 1: Request specific information or action.

Step 2: State reasoning and relevant information.

Step 3: State or restate details needed for compliance.

Step 4: Reiterate request, demonstrating confidence.

Mary Beth Alsopp
Soup Kitchen Chair
First Central Church
201 North Central Avenue
Southern Cross, Mississippi 64648

April 19, 2004

Reference: *Southern Cross Times*, April 19, 2004

Marilene Vanderhorn
Announcements Editor
Southern Cross Times
P.O. Box 8025
Southern Cross, Mississippi 64648

Dear Marilene Vanderhorn:

Today's *Times* published an incorrect date for the opening of First Central Church's Soup Kitchen; I'd like a correction made as soon as possible this week.

A copy of our original press release is attached for your information.

To help us recruit the volunteers still needed and to get word out to those who need it, please print a correction in the first weekday issue possible and again next Sunday. Many people who could be involved or who could use a good hot meal rely on word-of-mouth to hear about such events, so the sooner you can print a correction, the more our community stands to benefit.

Here is the correct information:

The grand opening of First Central Church's Soup Kitchen will be Sunday, May 3, from 11 a.m. to 2 p.m. The Soup Kitchen is located next to the church at 203 North Central Avenue. All in need are welcome; volunteers are still needed. For more information, call First Central Church at 655-8287.

Please call me if you need further information or are unable to comply with my request. You can reach me at 555-9871 (days) or 555-3599 (evenings).

Thanks for making this correction as quickly as possible.

Thank you,

Mary Beth Alsopp, Soup Kitchen Chair

Attachment: Original press release

Voicing an opinion

Hassan Sheheen
Rural Route 1092
Wilderness, Alaska 90505

February 16, 2004

John Copperfield
Photo Editor
Newsweak Magazine
P.O. Box 62409
Capital City, Maryland 21021

Dear John Copperfield:

Step 1: Request specific information or action.

I've noticed a troubling trend recently in the coverage that that *Newsweak Magazine* has given to issues related to the threat of terrorism. If your publication still strives to be a top source of no-nonsense, objective reporting, I encourage you to change your policy regarding your coverage of these issues.

Step 2: State reasoning and relevant information.

For quite some time now, *Newsweak* has seemed determined to present people who practice Islam in an unflattering, extremist light. As a devoted Muslim, I can tell you that the mainstream of our religion does not advocate the distorted and sick "holy war" notion that figures such as Osama Bin Laden have promoted. Your reporters need to research more carefully the sects of Islam that hold themselves responsible for terrorist acts.

That trend alone would be troubling enough. But now I'm seeing photographs of Muslim women in Middle Eastern countries, their faces shielded in veils and their arms grasping dirty children, which seem to present these people as objects of oddity, a spectacle to be marveled at by the reader. Such photographs are accompanied by headlines blaring the words such as *terrorist nation* or *hell in a land of extremism*.

Step 3: State or restate details needed for compliance.

If you're hoping to continue to attract an audience interested in an objective portrayal of real news, not propaganda, I fully expect to see *Newsweak* discontinue such irresponsible use of photographs and language.

Step 4: Reiterate request, demonstrating confidence.

With the line between news coverage and sensationalism becoming increasingly blurred, publications such as *Newsweak* have an obligation to report the news in accordance with its usual quality standards.

Sincerely,

Hassan Sheheen

cc: Roger Irvington, Editor in Chief

When previous requests fail, try Template 3

If you didn't get action from your Template 1 or 2 letters, use Template 3 to turn up the heat.

Demanding a correction or retraction

The Reverend Terrance Manley
United Church Federation
610 East 16th Avenue
Makepeace, Indiana 45678

August 6, 2004

Reference: Channel 6 News, August 3, 2004

CERTIFIED MAIL

Howard Neeley, Station Manager
Channel 6 News
310 W. Walker Avenue
Makepeace, Indiana 45678

Dear Mr. Neeley:

Step 1: State letter's purpose; acknowledge previous requests.

Because several phone calls over the last few days have failed to secure the promise of a retraction of comments made on your August 3 newscast, I am now writing to you, the station manager, to insist on such a retraction.

Step 2: Restate concern or request.

In the August 3 evening newscast, your reporter, Carole Ness, stated that United Church Federation members arriving at the scene of a violent murder "may have interfered with police attempts to apprehend the suspect." She further referred to the group of three people as "religious extremists" who, she suggested, had no business being there.

In fact, that United Church Federation's purpose in going to such gruesome scenes is to offer prayer and healing. We believe that through prayer, the systemic problem of violent crime in our cities can come to an end. The group is an *ad hoc* gathering of "members" who actually belong to churches, temples, and synagogues around the city. The Federation itself espouses no specific religious teachings other than a firm belief in the power of prayer.

Howard Neeley, Station Manager
August 6, 2004
page 2

As for Federation members interfering with police business at such scenes, it simply never happens. Federation members generally gather long after the police have left a scene of violence; when occasionally the police and our group are there simultaneously (as was the case in the four-hour ordeal that day), the relationship between the Federation and police is always one of mutual cooperation and respect.

Step 3: State expectations and possibly next steps.

I would encourage your reporter to talk to Police Chief Robert Gray to verify my position. His number is 321-8565.

Step 4: State or restate details needed for compliance.

Because television wields such power in influencing people's minds (as demonstrated by the flood of angry phone calls I've received in the last few days), I really must insist on a public retraction that includes only factual statements and an objective depiction of the Federation's activities.

Step 5: Reiterate request and (optionally) thank.

I would welcome a conversation with you or your reporter. My phone number, day or night, is 322-4575.

Thank you for your prompt attention to this matter. I look forward to hearing from you.

Sincerely,

Reverend Terrance Manley
United Church Federation

When to use Template 4

Use Template 4 to provide information when a persuasive approach isn't needed.

Announcing an event

The typical means for announcing an event for publication or broadcast is a press release. Press releases chosen for publication or broadcast are typically those that media personnel find easiest to use: They are essentially well-written (to the point and concise) and include all vital information.

When writing a press release, think like a journalist. Answer the journalist's "Seven Ws" as in Step 2 of your letter: Who, What, When, Where, Why, How, and How Much. (Okay the last two aren't Ws, but you get the idea.)

Step 1: Overview information or event letter will address.

Step 2: Provide information or describe event.

Step 3: Invite recipient to contact you and provide contact information.

Step 4: End with a lasting impression.

Mary Beth Alsopp
Soup Kitchen Chair
First Central Church
201 North Central Avenue
Southern Cross, Mississippi 64648

April 13, 2004

Elinor Nunnely, Program Director
KQSC-Radio
2112 North Meridian Street
Southern Cross, Mississippi 64648

Dear Elinor Nunnely:

For immediate release. Please announce the following not-for-profit event.

I'd be particularly grateful if you could announce this information during before- and after-work drive times so we may recruit the needed volunteers.

Here are the details:
The grand opening of First Central Church's Soup Kitchen will be Sunday, May 3, from 11 a.m. to 2 p.m. The Soup Kitchen is located next to the church at 203 North Central Avenue. All in need are welcome; volunteers are still needed. For more information, please call First Central Church at 655-8287.

For more information on this event, you can also call me at 555-9871 (days) or 555-3599 (evenings).

Thank you for your help in spreading the word to those in need and those who can help!

Sincerely,

Mary Beth Alsopp
Soup Kitchen Chair

Use Template 5 to say, "Thanks!"

To acknowledge someone's kindness or outstanding service you have received, use Template 5.

Thanking a reporter for fair coverage

Step 1: Acknowledge information or event.

Don't stop with a generic thank you. Describe what this individual did so your recognition comes across as more sincere.

Step 2: Elaborate as appropriate.

Step 3: End with a lasting impression.

Reverend Terrance Manley
United Church Federation
610 East 16th Avenue
Makepeace, Indiana 45678

August 18, 2004

Carole Ness, Senior Reporter
Channel 6 News
310 W. Walker Avenue
Makepeace, Indiana 45678

Dear Carole Ness:

Your report on last night's broadcast was a fine example of quality reporting.

Your depiction of United Church Federation's activities was both balanced and fair. I particularly valued your including the direct quotes from Police Chief Robert Gray.

You may never be fully aware of the benefits our city will reap by your quality work. I sincerely thank you.

May God bless,

Reverend Terrance Manley

cc: Howard Neeley, Station Manager

To tactfully deliver bad news use Template 6

If you want to maintain a long-standing relationship, deliver bad news, or decline participation, use a Template 6 letter. Template 6 "softens" bad news. However, if your news will not come as a big surprise or you haven't established a long-standing relationship, get to the point more quickly with Template 4 instead.

Canceling a long-held subscription

Step 1: Make general statement or restate request.

Step 2: Provide rationale behind negative response or bad news.

Step 3: State the negative response or bad news.

Step 4 An apology is not necessary here.

Step 5: End on a positive or encouraging note.

Kevin Longbear
Rural Route 1092
Wilderness, Alaska 90505

December 16, 2004

Roger Irvington
Editor-in-Chief
Newsweak Magazine
P.O. Box 62409
Capital City, Maryland 21021

Dear Roger Irvington:

Back in February I expressed my concerns to your photo editor about the direction I saw *Newsweak* heading with regard to irresponsible use of photography. A copy of my February letter is attached.

Since February, I've unfortunately seen continued use of the photographic techniques I described in that letter. What's more, *Newsweak*'s cover photos and cover designs now look even more like those of tabloid magazines, and its content strays further than ever into the territory of propaganda.

For these reasons, I have decided to end my subscription to a newsmagazine whose quality standards I have held in esteem for more than 20 years. Please consider this letter my official subscription cancellation.

The editorial staff of *Newsweak* is clearly quite talented. If the magazine's editorial policies ever get back to no-nonsense, objective news reporting, you can bet I'll reinstate my 20-year subscription.

Sincerely,

Kevin Longbear

cc: John Copperfield, Photo Editor
Attachment

Social Letters
and E-mails

Social letters are those addressed to friends, family, and acquaintances. You may write these letters for any purpose, from expressing greetings to raising a complaint with a neighbor. But because the relationship you have with the recipient of such a letter is important to you, you'll probably handle these letters with less formality and more (or less) intimacy.

Unless you're wanting simply to "journal" on paper to someone close to you ("It's been a long time…. Here's what we've been up to…."), social letters, too, have a purpose; structure them to best suit your purpose.

Social letters tend most often to follow Templates 1, 2, 4, or 5. Most social "good news" letters work best using Template 4 (providing information or describing an action you have taken or an event affecting you) or Template 5 (acknowledging an action someone else has taken or an event affecting that person). Even if the action or event you're discussing is "bad news" (a lost job or an illness, for instance), these templates work best.

Template 1 (requesting information or routine action from someone) is most appropriate for invitations or other routine requests. For requests that are less than routine, or those in which you might anticipate some resistance, use Template 2 (persuading someone to take action).

These letters should almost always be handwritten because of their highly personal, if not intimate, nature. How intimate you decide to make your letter depends on your words and tone. You'll also want to use one of the two social formats described in Chapter 5. (For more intimate letters, omit your own address.)

Social letter samples

Using Template 1

For invitations and other straightforward requests, use Template 1.

Inviting to an event or a get-together

Step 1: Request specific information or action.

Step 2: Cover relevant background and details.

Step 3: Contact information was provided with the return address.

Step 4: Reiterate action and/or thank.

> *1020 Chamberlain Way*
> *Hill Valley, South Carolina 75755*
> *March 18, 2004*
>
> *Dear Mr. and Mrs. Wilson,*
>
>   *Andrew K. Levinson and I will be married on Saturday, May 16, 2004. We would be honored if you could attend.*
>
>   *The ceremony will begin at 4 p.m. at the United Hebrew Congregation at 1338 North Main Street. A dinner reception will follow.*
>
>   *We hope you can join us to help celebrate this happy occasion.*
>
>   *Yours truly,*
>
>   *Rebecca Hochman*
>
> *Please respond by May 9, 2004*

Step 1: Request specific information or action.

Step 2: Cover relevant background and details.

Step 3: Providing contact information isn't necessary with close friends who know how to reach you.

Step 4: Reiterate action and/ or thank.

>   *August 14, 2004*
>
> *Dear Julia,*
>
>   *Alex and I were wondering if you, Eric, and the kids were free the weekend of September 12? The fall foliage should be beautiful then, and we'd love to have you spend the weekend with us down here in our "wilderness."*
>
>   *I think Alex would like to take the guys fishing, and I'd be happy taking a long drive through the country and finding a nice place to picnic, weather permitting.*
>
>   *I do hope you can join us for the weekend. Let us know.*
>
>   *Love from us all,*
>
>   *Jessica*

257

Making other straightforward requests

If you don't anticipate any resistance to your request, a Template 1 letter should be appropriate. If resistance is likely, a persuasive letter would be better. See page 259 for sample persuasive letters addressing the same situations.

Step 1: Request specific information or action.

Step 2: Cover relevant background and details.

Step 3: Providing contact information isn't necessary with close friends who know how to reach you.

Step 4: Reiterate action and/ or thank.

> *June 20, 2004*
>
> *Eliza,*
>
> *I can't tell you how relieved I am that Granddad made it through another bout with heart trouble. Let's pray he won't have any more.*
>
> *We had agreed to share expenses on the flower arrangement I had sent to his room, and here are the details on that.*
>
> *The entire cost, including delivery, was $42.87. Jim has agreed to chip in some too, so your share is only $14.29.*
>
> *You can get this to me however it's most convenient; a check by mail would be fine. Thanks!*
>
> *Love,*
>
> *Cheryl*

Step 1: Request specific information or action.

Step 2: Cover relevant background and details.

Step 3: Provide contact information.

Step 4: Reiterate action and/ or thank.

> *August 10, 2004*
>
> *Dear Joe,*
>
> *Hey, buddy, I need that drill back from you sometime in the next week.*
>
> *Amanda and I will be in and out running errands most of the weekend; if you come by and we're not there, leave it in the garage, okay? (Call me if you've forgotten the trick to get in.)*
>
> *Thanks, Joe. Say, how do those new doors look?*
>
> *Alex*

For less-than-routine requests, use Template 2

You may occasionally have a reason to write a letter persuading a friend or acquaintance to take action. Maybe your best friend needs to be persuaded to take a trip with you or a close neighbor has failed to return your lawnmower after repeated requests. These letters call for a Template 2 approach.

Making not-so-straightforward requests

Step 1: Request specific information or action.

Step 2: State reasoning and relevant information.

Step 3: State or restate details needed for compliance.

Step 4: Reiterate request, demonstrating confidence.

> *June 20, 2004*
>
> *Eliza,*
>
> *I can't tell you how relieved I am that Granddad made it through another bout with heart trouble. Let's pray he won't have any more.*
>
> *Would you mind sharing expenses on the flower arrangement I had sent to his room? I didn't have a chance to ask you about this ahead of time, but I took the liberty of signing the card "Love from your grandkids."*
>
> *The entire cost, including delivery, was $42.87. Jim has agreed to chip in some too, so your share would be only $14.29. If you can't or would rather not chip in, let me know either way, okay? Jim and I can handle it alone if you need us to.*
>
> *Send me a check or call me as soon as you can. Thanks!*
>
> *Love,*
>
> *Cheryl*

Step 1: Request specific information or action.

Step 2: State reasoning and relevant information.

Step 3: State or restate details needed for compliance.

Step 4: Reiterate request, demonstrating confidence.

> *August 10, 2004*
>
> *Dear Joe,*
>
> *Do you think I could get that drill back I loaned you last month?*
>
> *Amanda and I are considering our own home-remodeling project, and I just remembered that I loaned you my drill. We want to install bigger windows in the kitchen—if, that is, we can find some we like. (We've been shopping for the last three weeks solid!)*
>
> *I don't imagine we'll make any final decisions until next weekend, so if you can get the drill back to me by, say, next Sunday, I'd appreciate it!*
>
> *Thanks, Joe. Say, how do those new doors look?*
>
> *Alex*

An alternative to complaining: Requesting information

Complaining to someone with whom you have a more personal or long-standing relationship can be a delicate matter. If you've decided what the other person can do to make things right, use the persuasive approach (Template 2). For instance, instead of "complaining" to Joe about not returning his drill (second letter, page 249), Alex instead tried to persuade Joe to return it.

Even if you haven't decided what would make things right in a situation, you may still want to consider a persuasive approach—persuade the other person to work the problem out with you.

Step 1: Request specific information or action.

Step 2: State reasoning and relevant information.

Step 3: State or restate details needed for compliance.

Step 4: Reiterate request, demonstrating confidence.

September 18, 2004

Dear Bob,

Jill and I need your help with an ongoing frustration we've been experiencing. Could we talk about landscaping decisions either of our families make that affect the space between our houses?

Please don't misunderstand: We have enjoyed the evergreens you planted in the "no man's land" between our houses. They're very attractive and give both of our homes additional privacy. We were thinking, however, of planting wildflowers there before the trees went in. Because we've always had difficulty mowing that uneven area, we thought wildflowers would make it easier to maintain.

You and May have been wonderful neighbors, and we hate to even bring this landscape issue up; I know, however, that issues can fester and grow between people when they don't talk about them. We value our relationship with you both too much to let that happen.

Can we talk further about this and other landscaping issues affecting both of our houses? I'll try to catch up with you sometime this weekend to get your thoughts on this issue.

Thanks for your understanding,

Frank Ford

In social situations, avoid Template 3 letters

In social situations, when relationships are especially important to maintain, you'll probably never write a Template 3 letter to demand action. Template 3 letters can come across as harsh in a social context and potentially damaging to important relationships. If your routine request or persuasive letter doesn't do the trick, you might have better luck with a follow-up phone call or visit.

If you do choose to communicate further in writing, handle your next communication as a persuasive, rather than a demanding, letter. Write using a tone most likely to elicit a response. Ask for what you want directly, but in a more casual, friendly manner, and a little humor never hurts: "Hey, pal, what about that lawnmower? When can I get it back from you?"

And if you can do anything to help your friend (neighbor, family member) to save face about the situation, do so. "Hey, I'm planning to be in your neighborhood on Saturday; mind if I drop by and get it from you then?"

Creating a friendly follow-up letter when your first request hasn't been met is possible; but again, in these situations, letters are usually a poor substitute for a phone call or visit.

For most social letters, use Templates 4 or 5

Many social letters are written to convey good news. Write these most easily using Template 4 (to provide information or describe an event) or Template 5 (to acknowledge information or an event). Template 4 letters follow. Template 5 letters begin on page 267 with "Accepting an Invitation."

Announcing a graduation

Step 1: Overview information or event letter will address.

Step 2: Provide information or describe event.

Step 3: Inviting recipient to contact you and providing contact information isn't appropriate if you do not expect follow-up contact.

Step 4: End with a lasting impression.

> *44 Emington Way*
> *Terrace, Utah 98987*
> *May 14, 2004*
>
> *Dear Mr. Elliott,*
>
> *I am pleased to announce that on May 9, 2004, I was graduated from Purdue University with a degree in nursing. I'll be starting work in critical care at the Veteran's Hospital in just a few weeks.*
>
> *Thank you for your interest over the years in my education and other endeavors. I've always valued your guidance and support.*
>
> *Sincerely,*
>
> *April Alexander*

Announcing a move

Step 1: Overview information or event letter will address.

Step 2: Provide information or describe event.

Step 3: Invite recipient to contact you and provide contact information.

Step 4: End with a lasting impression.

June 5, 2004

Dear Ed and Joan,

Hey, we've moved! Kelly's work has taken us north to Minneapolis, Minnesota.

After much debate, Kelly accepted a great job at Best Bet's headquarters here. It was a good move for both of us (I have family here), and we're looking forward to everything Minneapolis has to offer, except perhaps subzero winter temperatures.

Please make note of our new address and phone number:

Kelly and Tim Hancock
18377 Lakeview Boulevard
Minneapolis, Minnesota 55488
612/555-1154

Take care of yourselves, and consider visiting us soon, okay?

Love from both of us,

Tim

Announcing an engagement

Step 1: Overview information or event letter will address.

Step 2: Provide information or describe event.

Step 3: Inviting recipient to contact you and providing contact information isn't appropriate if you do not expect follow-up contact.

Step 4: End with a lasting impression.

February 10, 2004

Dear Samantha,

I wanted you to be one of the first to know some happy news. Larry Eldridge and I are engaged to be married!

Larry and I have known each other for just over a year, and he's like no one I've ever met before. He's creative and funny—I'm sure you'll like him.

We haven't set a date yet, but we're thinking maybe early fall. We'll keep you posted.

I can't wait for you to meet Larry!

Love,

Michelle

Announcing a marriage

Step 1: Overview information or event letter will address.

Step 2: Provide information or describe event.

Step 3: Inviting recipient to contact you and providing contact information isn't appropriate if you do not expect follow-up contact.

Step 4: End with a lasting impression.

5077 Eagle's View Terrace
Desert, New Mexico 14125
February 25, 2004

Dear Terry and Hannah,

I'm delighted to let you know that Janet and I were married in her hometown of Houston, Texas, on Saturday, February 7, 2004.

The ceremony was small and informal, just our style. We'll be settling in Amarillo, near my family and most of our friends. Janet will continue to be known as Janet Tomlinson.

We're both very happy and look forward to our new life together!

Love to you both,

Bill

Announcing a birth

Step 1: Overview information or event letter will address.

Step 2: Provide information or describe event.

Step 3: Inviting recipient to contact you and providing contact information isn't appropriate if you do not expect follow-up contact.

Step 4: End with a lasting impression.

June 8, 2004

Dear Jane and Matt,

Brian and I are happy to announce the birth of our first child, a daughter, Amanda Elizabeth.

Mandy, as we'll call her, was born on April 30 at 2:35 a.m. and weighed 7 pounds, 9 ounces.

We're all well and gradually adjusting to this new family of three.

All the best to your family,

Joy Templeton

Announcing an adoption

Step 1: Overview information or event letter will address.

Step 2: Provide information or describe event.

Step 3: Inviting recipient to contact you and providing contact information isn't appropriate if you do not expect follow-up contact.

Step 4: End with a lasting impression.

> *73 Dairy Way*
> *Evans, Wisconsin 36332*
> *October 28, 2004*
>
> *Dear Mr. and Mrs. Barrett,*
>
> *Please allow us to share some good news. We're parents for a second time! On October 10, 2004, we adopted our second child, Joseph Patrick. He was just one week old when we brought him home.*
>
> *His older sister, Katie, isn't quite sure what to make of Joseph yet, but she already seems quite fond of him.*
>
> *We're as happy as we can possibly be!*
>
> *Kind regards,*
>
> *Chuck and Evelyn Tudor*

Announcing a divorce

While generally not cause for celebration, a divorce might require an announcement letter. Tactfully explaining a change of address or name change to friends or family can be a touchy, but helpful, reason for a letter.

Unless you know your letter's recipients very well, these letters are best kept short and report only critical details in an unemotional way. Template 5 works best.

Step 1: Overview information or event letter will address.

Step 2: Provide information or describe event.

Step 3: Invite recipient to contact you and provide contact information.

Step 4: End with a lasting impression.

> *October 16, 2004*
>
> *Dear Joe and Katie,*
>
> *Eric and I were unfortunately divorced last month, and I'm now living at a new address:*
>
> *8610 East 98th Street*
> *Ellotsville, Florida 11211*
>
> *The children will be living with me here. I've also gone back to using my maiden name, "Weisberg."*
>
> *I know I speak for Eric when I say we have both valued your friendship over the years and hope we can keep in touch.*
>
> *Love,*
>
> *Ellie*

Sending holiday greetings

Most people appreciate receiving holiday greetings—so long as they show some measure of restraint; a typed two-page "newsletter" accompanying your Christmas card might be a little wearing on your loved ones. You would also do well to include only information you can anticipate your letter's readers will want to hear about. Paragraph after paragraph about your job might not express the holiday cheer you're hoping for.

What should your letter include? The people who care about you do want to know about those significant events in your family's life: health, births, deaths, favorite activities, trips, and significant milestones. But keep these tips in mind:

- Keep to the topics most important to you.

- Share a detail or two instead of making general statements. Say, "We hiked the park's two highest peaks," rather than "Our trip was adventurous." Say, "Our new granddaughter has her mother's big, blue eyes and her father's smile," rather than "Our new granddaughter is beautiful."

- Share accomplishments without boasting.

- Keep you letter as brief as possible.

Is a photocopied letter acceptable? People express different views about receiving the typed, photocopied letters many people send with holiday cards. Staunch traditionalists would never send such letters but prefer instead to write personal, if shorter, messages to their loved ones. Most people understand, however, that major holidays are busy correspondence times; and a photocopied letter seems a reasonable way to communicate life's important events to many people at once.

But be sure to include some personal message, even if it's just a quick line or message informally written onto the end of the typed letter. A handwritten message communicates that you thought about each recipient and are sending warm wishes personally.

Step 1: Overview information or event letter will address.

Step 2: Provide information or describe event.

Step 3: Inviting recipient to contact you and providing contact information isn't needed if recipient knows how to contact you.

Step 4: End with a lasting impression.

December 15, 2004

Dear Family and Friends,

Holiday greetings from our family to yours!

This year has been a busy one for the Jameses. Christen, as you know, started college at Tennessee State this fall; Steven and I have missed her horribly and have had a bit of a difficult time adjusting to the proverbial "empty nest." What do we do with our time now? Our older daughter, Amy, has been a real support to us during this time. She and her husband, Tom, who live just 30 minutes away, celebrated their second wedding anniversary with a new baby—our third grandbaby! Born April 10, Amanda Erin came into the world with Tom's intense red hair and Amy's blue eyes. Big brother Trevor seems crazy about his little sister.

The twins are also well: John's still in California working as a computer technician and claims he has the best job in the world. Alan and his wife, Debbie, prefer the country life and have started a small organic farm on the outskirts of Indianapolis. Their 2-year-old daughter, Emily, continues to be a great joy to both her parents and Steven and me, who spoil her terribly.

Steven still enjoys his work with the university, and I've been considering part-time secretarial work to occupy my time. I'm still very involved as a volunteer with the public schools, which I'd like to continue, but I'm also feeling an urge to reorient myself to the business world. With Christen away at school, I'm beginning to consider some exciting new prospects for my working life. Steven, bless him, supports any new idea I have, no matter how fleeting.

And our health has never been better, I'm happy to report. Steven has me jogging (okay, walking) with him in the mornings, and we've both managed to lose a little weight.

That's largely what's been happening at our house. We'd very much like to hear what's been happening at yours.

Happy Holidays!

Elizabeth and Steven James

Tom and Jennifer,

Please drop us a line when it's convenient, and please accept our warmest wishes for a happy holiday season and year ahead.

Elizabeth and Steven

Accepting an invitation

Because accepting an invitation is typically another way of acknowledging an event affecting someone else, use Template 5 for these letters.

Step 1: Acknowledge information or event.

Step 2: No elaboration is needed here.

Step 3: End with a lasting impression.

---

1 S. Broadway Avenue
Hill Valley, South Carolina 75755
May 6, 2004

Dear Rebecca,

What wonderful news! Jerold and I would be pleased to join you and your fiancé for your marriage ceremony and dinner reception on May 16.

Count on two of us. We're looking forward to it!

Kind regards,

Allison Wilson

Step 1: Acknowledge information or event.

Step 2: Elaborate as appropriate.

Step 3: End with a lasting impression.

August 22, 2004

Dear Jessica,

We'd be delighted to join you for a weekend in the "wilderness!"

Edie has a Girl Scout outing that weekend, so she unfortunately won't be joining us. She's quite content, though, to spend the rest of the weekend, after her outing, at a girlfriend's house.

Eric and the boys are certainly up for fishing. I say we let them deal with the hooks and worms while you and I take ourselves on a picnic! It'll be fun to catch up.

I'll call you next weekend to discuss the details.

Looking forward to it!

Julia

Congratulating on a graduation

Step 1:
Acknowledge
information or
event.

Step 2:
Elaborate as
appropriate.

Step 3: End
with a lasting
impression.

23 Westbelt Way
St. Lawrence, Missouri 63333-1111
June 5, 2004

Dear John,

I understand from Tim Jeffries that you have graduated from Silverton College. What an accomplishment! Congratulations.

Way back when you helped my husband and me with those occasional odd jobs, I knew that your dedication to excellence would help you succeed with whatever you chose to do.

Jim and I wish you the very best as you begin your life as a working professional.

Fondly,

Julie Robinson

Step 1:
Acknowledge
information or
event.

Step 2:
Elaborate as
appropriate.

Step 3: End
with a lasting
impression.

May 29, 2004

Dear April,

Hey, congratulations! I'm really proud of you, April, for obtaining your nursing degree from Purdue.

As a Purdue grad myself, I know something of how hard you worked to get that degree. You should be quite proud of yourself.

Best of luck to you,

Charles Elliott

Congratulating on a promotion, award, or other achievement

Step 1:
Acknowledge
information or
event.

Step 2:
Elaborate as
appropriate.

Step 3: End
with a lasting
impression.

779 Pine Way
Sea Water, Washington 46464
December 9, 2004

Dear Bonnie,

I was thrilled to read in this week's paper that you're being honored for your work with the homeless.

Your selfless dedication to such an important cause, donating countless hours participating in everything from home construction to home financing to life-skills support, is indeed admirable.

Congratulations on receiving an honor you so clearly deserve!

Regards,

Jim

Step 1:
Acknowledge
information or
event.

Step 2:
Elaborate as
appropriate.

Step 3: End
with a lasting
impression.

September 30, 2004

Dear Julie,

Congratulations on your new job! We ran into Janis at the grocery store, who mentioned your great news.

The job sounds like a real challenge—one I feel certain you'll find rewarding. (You always did enjoy a good challenge!)

I wish you a smooth transition into life at Tomlin Electronics and much success in the years to come!

Blessings to you,

Jill Thomas

Congratulating on an engagement or a marriage

Step 1:
Acknowledge
information or
event.

Step 2:
Elaborate as
appropriate.

Step 3: End
with a lasting
impression.

88 Rockfire Road
Angel, South Dakota 32141
March 16, 2004

Dear Sarah,

We noticed your engagement announcement in Sunday's newspaper. What wonderful news!

As you know, your mother and father have been dear friends of ours for years, and we were delighted to learn of this latest cause for celebration in your family.

Our very best regards to you and your fiancé.

Very sincerely yours,

Tim and Judy Eagleton

Step 1:
Acknowledge
information or
event.

Step 2:
Elaborate as
appropriate.

Step 3: End
with a lasting
impression.

66 Musicians Lane
Big Break, Tennessee 73737
July 26, 2004

Dear Tom and Terri,

I hear congratulations are in order! I was so happy to hear that the two of you were married last month. I can't think of a better-suited couple (except for perhaps Ellie and me).

Best wishes for a long, happy life together.

Fondly,

Al Stevenson

Congratulating on a birth or an adoption

Step 1:
Acknowledge
information or
event.

Step 2:
Elaborate as
appropriate.

Step 3: End
with a lasting
impression.

June 16, 2004

Dear Joy and Brian,

   Matt and I were thrilled to hear about the birth of your daughter, Amanda Elizabeth.

   Children add so much joy to our lives, and we were thrilled to hear the two of you have decided to "take the plunge" into parenthood.

   Please accept our congratulations on this happy occasion.

                              Kind regards,

                              Jane Simpson

Step 1:
Acknowledge
information or
event.

Step 2:
Elaborate as
appropriate.

Step 3: End
with a lasting
impression.

1776 Independence Way
Harrisburg, Pennsylvania 32121
November 10, 2004

Dear Chuck and Evelyn,

   Congratulations on the arrival of your son, Joseph Patrick, into your family.

   Please accept this welcoming gift on his behalf along with our warm wishes for a joyful life together.

   We wish all of you the very best on this happy occasion.

                              Sincerely yours,

                              Kory and Patricia Barrett

271

Thanking for a gift or other kindness

Acknowledging a kind act someone has taken on your behalf calls for a Template 5 letter.

Step 1:
Acknowledge information or event.

Step 2:
Elaborate as appropriate.

Step 3: End with a lasting impression.

52 Crackerjack Hill
Raysdell, Louisiana 91919

June 30, 2004

Dear Clara,

I really enjoyed dinner at your place last Saturday night. You have lots of interesting friends! Jamey and I, in fact, have talked about getting together for lunch sometime. We seem to have a lot in common.

Thanks so much for including me. You've really helped to make my adjustment to a new town a little easier.

Cordially,

Brenda

Step 1:
Acknowledge information or event.

Step 2:
Elaborate as appropriate.

Step 3: End with a lasting impression.

September 15, 2004

Dear Aunt Syl and Uncle Rob,

Your generous $100 gift was so thoughtful. As you suggested, Jim and I do need a lot of things to set up our new household, and your gift will certainly come in handy. (We're thinking it will give us a good start on some pots and pans!)

Okay, I know what you're thinking: "What's Edie going to do with pots and pans?" Well, Aunt Syl, I married a man who can cook!

Once we have a functioning kitchen, we would very much like the two of you to join us for a nice meal. I promise to let Jim do the cooking.

We'll be in touch soon,

Edie

Sending get-well wishes for an illness or accident

Template 5 is useful for acknowledging even bad news affecting someone else.

Step 1:
Acknowledge
information or
event.

Step 2:
Elaborate as
appropriate.

Step 3: End
with a lasting
impression.

November 2, 2004

Dear Aunt Syl,

I was so sorry to hear about Uncle Rob's recent hospitalization. Mother told me that he'll need solid bed rest for several weeks. I bet he's going crazy having to stay put.

Aunt Syl, I happen to have a little time on my hands lately, so if you'll accept this, I'd like to come by next week to help out in any way I can. (I'll even do some cooking, if you can stand it.) Would that be all right? I'll call you before I come by.

You and Uncle Rob have always looked out for me, and I'd very much like the opportunity to return the favor.

I love you both,

Edie

Step 1:
Acknowledge
information or
event.

Step 2:
Elaborate as
appropriate.

Step 3: End
with a lasting
impression.

May 4, 2004

Dear Minnie,

I was shocked to hear from Jean Thomas about your accident last week. But I'm thrilled you'll fully recover in time.

Jean mentioned that I might be allowed to visit you in a few days, so plan on seeing me one day next week after work.

Please know that I am thinking of you and praying for your speedy and complete recovery.

I miss you around here,

Julie

June 23, 2004

Step 1:
Acknowledge
information or
event.

Dear Michael,

So you're in bed with mono. Lucky break, I figure. But did you have to go to such lengths just to avoid the annual McCoy reunion? Seriously, I'll really miss you this Sunday.

Step 2:
Elaborate as
appropriate.

I'd come for a visit, but I hear you're contagious. I promise I'll call, okay? Besides, you'll probably be dying to know what happened at the reunion.

Step 3: End
with a lasting
impression.

Until then, I'll try to pull our regular antics without you. It won't be the same, but I'll do my best. You work on getting well, and I'll check in on you next week.

Hang in there,

Phil

Sending support for a serious or terminal illness, or accident

January 11, 2004

Step 1:
Acknowledge
information or
event.

Dear Yvonne,

I was so sorry to hear about your illness and hospitalization. I am encouraged, though, to know that you're receiving good care and lots of support.

Step 2:
Elaborate as
appropriate.

I was in the hospital only once in my life, and I remember just how difficult it was to be confined to bed with little to do. Besides that, I didn't feel like doing much anyway. Could you use some company? I'll do my best to get by in the next few days for a visit.

Step 3: End
with a lasting
impression.

Please know that my thoughts and prayers are with you during this difficult time, and if I can do anything for you—anything at all—please ask.

We all miss you,

Julie

Sending condolences

Condolence letters are probably the single most difficult letters to write. Many well-intentioned people handle them poorly and actually offend rather than comfort the person grieving. Here, for instance, are wishes that should *never* appear in a condolence letter:

- Charlie's in a "better place," "heaven," "with God," or otherwise "better off."

- "God chose to take" Jamie or Jamie's "doing God's work now."

- At least your baby "won't experience the hardships of life," or "didn't live a long life of pain."

- Don't worry: "you'll see Tommy again in heaven."

Someone grieving does not need to be talked out of the grief. He or she needs comforting ("I'm sorry for your loss"), but the reality is that the loved one is no longer here.

Avoid, too, trying to encourage the person back to a place of normalcy. Different people experience grief differently, and it is often a slow process. Avoid wishes such as:

- "When will you be coming back" to church?

- We "hope you'll be feeling better soon," or I "hope you're better now three months after the funeral."

- "Are you over his death?"

- "Is it getting any easier?"

Here are a few suggestions for better condolence letters:
Think what you would find comforting if you were the person grieving. Say that.

- Say a kind word about the deceased: "He always made me smile;" "She was always there when I needed her."

- Tell the person grieving about an experience you had with the deceased that made an impression on you.

- Don't ask questions about the accident, illness, or other circumstances of the death. Your purpose is to comfort.

- Try to keep your letter short. Say what you're feeling very simply and stop. You'll never "fix" the grief, so don't try.

- Don't make offers you're not prepared to keep: Will you really follow up in a few weeks with a dinner invitation?

- Then, for heaven's sake, follow up with any offers of assistance or promises to call!

Step 1: Acknowledge information or event.

Step 2: Elaborate as appropriate.

Step 3: End with a lasting impression.

April 22, 2004

Dear Randy and Barbara,

My husband and I just learned of Tim's death. We are still in shock and so deeply sorry.

Tim was such a fun, creative boy. When he and Jason played together as small children, they were always into something really different and a lot of fun. Jason wasn't the only one who so enjoyed having him around our house.

Please know that our thoughts and prayers are with you during this difficult time.

We'll miss him,

Cecilia and Charles

Step 1: Acknowledge information or event.

Step 2: Elaborate as appropriate.

Step 3: End with a lasting impression.

December 18, 2004

Dear Francine,

My thoughts are with you at this sad time. I know how close you and your mother were, and I can only imagine what you must be going through right now.

When I lost my father, I found it helpful to hear what other people thought of him during his life. As perhaps you already know, I think your mom was one of the kindest, wisest, most thoughtful people I've ever known. I'll never forget that time, when you and I were teenagers, when she came to my rescue after my first fender-bender. I was so upset—so sure my own parents would kill me—but she helped me calm down and deal responsibly with the situation.

Although you and I are thousands of miles apart right now, please know that I'm praying for your comfort. And if I can do anything at all for you, please ask. I'm only a phone call away.

Love,

Diane

February 13, 2004

Step 1:
Acknowledge
information or
event.

Step 2:
Elaborate as
appropriate.

Step 3: End
with a lasting
impression.

Dear Margaret,

    We spoke only briefly at the viewing, and I would really like to share some words I hope you'll find comforting.

    While I didn't know Matthew well, you two seemed so good together, so spontaneous and full of life. The number of people at the viewing is testimony to just how attracted others were to you two. You always gave other people so much of yourselves.

    The thought of losing my own husband is too painful even to contemplate; I can't begin to know what you're feeling. But I hope, somehow, that you can remember how others love you and that you can find comfort in that.

                   My prayers are with you,

                     Tara

Thanking for condolences

May 12, 2004

Step 1:
Acknowledge
information or
event.

Step 2:
Elaborate as
appropriate.

Step 3: End
with a lasting
impression.

Dear Cecilia and Charles,

    Randy and I cannot express how much your note meant to us. It's been a few years since Jason and Tim played together as boys, and the memories of their friendship really warmed our hearts.

    Your kind words about Tim were very thoughtful. Please give Jason our best, and thanks again for writing.

                     Warmly,

                 Randy and Barbara

Step 1:
Acknowledge information or event.

Step 2:
Elaborate as appropriate.

Step 3: End with a lasting impression.

January 4, 2004

Dear Diane,

Thank you so much for writing, Diane. Your words about Mom meant a lot. As you suspect, I will miss her terribly.

And thank you, too, for your prayers. I believe prayers have more power than we can ever understand.

I think of you often,

Francine

Step 1:
Acknowledge information or event.

Step 2:
Elaborate as appropriate.

Step 3: End with a lasting impression.

February 27, 2004

Dear Tara,

I really appreciated receiving your note last week. Your thoughtful words and reassurance were, in fact, comforting. I am grateful that so many people over the years have offered their love and support to both Matthew and me.

Thank you for offering me yours,

Margaret

Soften bad news with Template 6

When you must decline a social request or convey bad news, Template 6 is the most appropriate way to go. Unlike all other templates, Template 6 works up to the point gradually rather than stating it immediately. This approach makes the most sense simply because it "softens the blow" and encourages your recipient to keep reading until all the facts are presented.

Declining an invitation

Step 1: Make general state-ment or restate request.

Step 2: Provide rationale behind negative response or bad news.

Step 3: State the negative response or bad news.

Step 4: Apolo-gize, if warranted.

Step 5: End on a positive or encouraging note.

1 S. Broadway Avenue
Hill Valley, South Carolina 75755
May 6, 2004

Dear Rebecca,

What wonderful news! I know you and Andrew have dated for quite some time, and I'm thrilled to see the two of you taking this important step. Your mother tells me he's a wonderful fellow.

Mr. Wilson and I have been planning a once-in-a-lifetime vacation to Europe for months. Unfortunately, our trip means we will be of the country on May 16.

We're so sorry we won't be able to be present for your important event.

Please accept our wishes for a wonderful day and a long life together. The enclosed check is to help with anything you need as you begin your life together.

Kind regards,

Allison Wilson

Step 1: Make general state-ment or restate request.

Step 2: Provide rationale behind negative response or bad news.

Step 3: State the negative response or bad news.

Step 4: An apology is not necessary here.

Step 5: End on a positive or encouraging note.

August 22, 2004

Dear Jessica,

How tempting was your offer to spend the weekend watching the leaves turn! I could sure use a nice "wilderness" getaway.

That weekend is a particularly busy one for us. I've volunteered to chaperone an outing with Edie's Girl Scout troop, and it's Eric's weekend for the Reserves. Looks like we'll have to take a raincheck.

Maybe we can plan for another weekend or even have you visit us up here. We can't offer much in the way of trees, but I'd sure enjoy seeing you guys.

I'll call you after our busy weekend, okay?

Love to you all,

Julia

Delivering bad news

Step 1: Make general statement or restate request.

Step 2: Provide rationale behind negative response or bad news.

Step 3: State the negative response or bad news.

Step 4: An apology is not necessary here.

Step 5: End on a positive or encouraging note.

3030 Seashell Lane
Sea Isle, Rhode Island 16112
April 30, 2004

Dear Alicia,

As you know, my husband, Thomas, and I have been searching for the perfect "match" in an all-summer sitter for our children, Raymond and Molly.

In the past few weeks, we've interviewed literally dozens of prospective sitters, most of whom were extremely well-qualified to do the job. You were certainly one of these.

I'm sure you can imagine that this has been a major decision for my husband and me. In addition to seeking someone with excellent qualifications and references, we were looking for someone who demonstrated the best "chemistry" with our special-needs children. (You may remember our mentioning this as the reason we had you meet and spend a few minutes with the children when you came for an interview.)

We have decided to hire an older woman who met our high standards and also lives very close to my place of business. This was an added bonus we never dreamed we would find.

Thomas and I sincerely thank you for your time, effort, and patience as we worked through this lengthy but important interview process.

We were very impressed with your skills. You're a very impressive young lady, and we wish you the very best in all your future pursuits.

Please give your parents our best,

Evelyn Mayfair

Delivering bad news with an apology

Step 1: Make general statement or restate request.

Step 2: Provide rationale behind negative response or bad news.

Step 3: State the negative response or bad news.

Step 4: Apologize, if warranted.

Step 5: End on a positive or encouraging note.

September 1, 2004

Dear Alex,

I know you're wondering why I haven't returned your drill.

It's a bit of a long story, but if you'll bear with me, I'll explain. I used the drill to install the new doors, which really look fantastic, by the way. Then another project came up: installing shelves in our garage. Elaine has begged me for shelves to help contain some of the clutter out there, so I took the opportunity to take on that project too.

Well, that project went fine, and I used the new shelves right away, to temporarily store your drill alongside my own electric equipment, which I had been storing in the basement.

To make a long story short, the garage door was inadvertently left open one afternoon about two weeks ago, and well, buddy, I'm afraid your drill was stolen along with about $500 of my own equipment.

I'm really sorry we were so careless. And I also apologize for not calling you when it happened; I didn't realize until I got your letter that more than my equipment had been stolen!

I'll replace your drill, of course; I just haven't had the chance to get out to get one. Now that I know you need it almost immediately, I'll get it to you by the end of the week.

Thanks for your understanding,

Joe

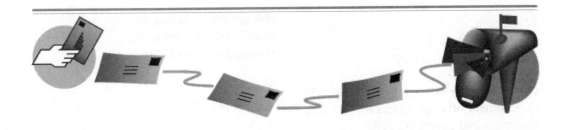

Index

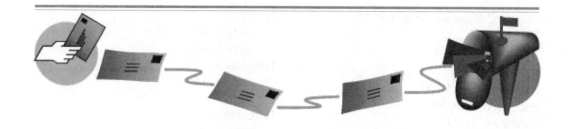

Index of Sample Letters and E-mail Messages